Introduction

A brief explanation of the cover page would be useful. Why a fog, with things, barely seen? Well, that is the life of a person with depression. Not only do they increase the fogginess both inside themselves, but they also live in a medication lethargy. During their worst downers, they hide from the world too afraid to go out except for the bare necessities, doctors, shrinks, psychologists prescriptions.They even go so far as to have their groceries and medications delivered to them.

I knew a lady in her late 40's and 50's, Sxxxx for many years. She had suffered from depression most of her life and had been undergoing therapy since her 20's. She smoked like a chimney because of her condition and the deeper she sank into it, the more she smoked. Had suffered bouts of addiction with alcohol, and she was throughout her life on medication. The unfortunate thing about her medications was that like anything one takes for too long a period, the efficacy lessened, and she had to switch to other pills for relief. The pill cure was a constant try, suffer the side effects and change till real, or more often the case temporary relief happened. A few days ago another sufferer posted on Google+ regarding this very medication failure.

She had attempted suicide several times before I knew her and tried twice while here in this state with one known attempt and save interstate and another milder one there, during which she saved herself.

The second to last time I heard from her was "Don't save me. Don't ring my daughter!" Had gotten a fairly cold response after alerting her via email during the first interstate attempt. One of the comments was strange as she told me to "Go find another helpless woman and use her."

I can't see how being on call 24/7, whenever she needed support over some six years classified me as a predator. "You'll never know what I will do from now on, and that will hurt you". She was blaming me for saving her previously, blaming me for being concerned about her, blaming me for having a healthy life and talking and sharing it as friends do, while she became more and more secluded and sickly. She was possibly, blaming me for adding one female friend and spending time helping her?

My last conversation, because I couldn't intuitively feel her was that she had done the deed when I called, and it turned into another "It's your fault and how dare you, feel sad." She seemed to think I would go into my depression knowing she might, off herself. Yes, I was sad she had let her lifeline go that I had persevered with for so many years!

In the end, it sometimes comes down to not being able to do anything else, because of the distance, the ladies decision and my helplessness legally speaking if I alerted the authorities incorrectly and so I just, let go. No longer feel the psychic connection we had, but that had also happened when she was in extreme depression, so am hopeful. Have been getting the crying feeling again when she was in turmoil, along with silence when I answer the phone several times a week. Have called her name on occasion but no response to date.

While living here, on the other side of town, she had utilised the consultative abilities of three psychologists, one a specialist, along with her GP visits monthly for her meds. The first psychologist I knew about had to release her due to ill health after some seven years. She had been going to her for a long time and was exceedingly distraught losing her. The woman I believe had taken on the mothering, nurturing aspect.

Thinking back, I now understand why she turned on me. Somehow she felt betrayed by me as she had by her psychologist, especially after I began helping my Italian paesana.

In some respects I took on some of the psychologist's role, consoling and counselling her after that.

She agreed to my trying specific shaman techniques. I began to loosen her body with massage, and she went from the tense, taught state she was in, into, by the time I had finished almost relaxed. Most of the pain spots had been lost or reduced to manageable and or minor, and she was living a reasonably comfortable lifestyle even though she was going through a worker's compensation claim and fight with her employers, with my help.

She then found herself a clinical psychologist, and although he diagnosed a few things similar to what I had, after the first few productive sessions it began sounding like they were fighting each other. He was not listening to what she was saying, and on more than one occasion I had to talk her down or go and see her to calm her from her suicidal inclinations. She was highly prone to male negativeness, and he definitely, rubbed her the wrong way.

After one session she decided to follow my advice and dump the antagonist and moved to another, a female, mothering type which she seemed to need and responded to better.

At the same time while she saw these I was also using Gestalt, Zen intuitive words and my intuited past, memory images therapy, Huna intuitive breathe sounds, the Sandman, a symbolic magic technique for sleep therapy, other alternatives, sand therapies and acupressure, along with closed eye memory recall as I massaged.

All of the above managed to get her back to work and work capably after being severely depressed previously from battles with several abusive supervisors both male and female. A recent comment about her workplace still has it as a toxic employee environment.

My shaman spirit animal transfer gave her sufficient confidence to get herself a better job interstate after a few months back at work.

I had wanted to continue with her therapy for several months more to ensure she fully stabilised, but she transferred interstate. She then commenced a slow downward spiral due to the pressure of the job, no training, and a fall and concussion in the carpark at work causing headaches which she didn't report and so couldn't claim.

However, I also understood that our relationship was getting too close to her fears about how close emotionally, she could be with a man, and so I let the bird fly the nest.

Although I have no qualifications, I found she was recovering better with the methods I was employing than the consultations and pills they were and had been giving her forever, and so I offer these techniques in the hope they may help you or the people you know.

Chapter 1
The Human Body

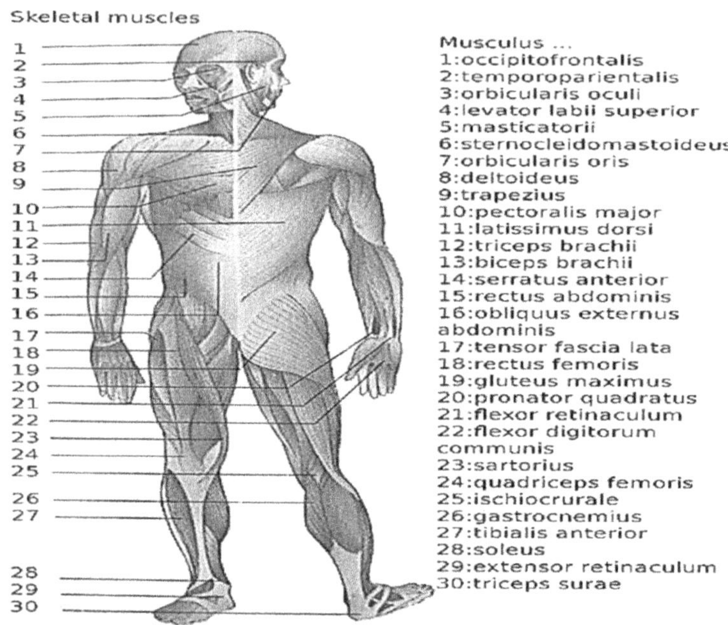

Trauma and tension get locked into the muscles of our bodies, generally the worst ones at birth, and the first few formative years. Different muscle positions reflect different emotional traumas. However, constant worry can increase tension in the body promoting muscle stiffness, with the corresponding pain severity increase following. The number of times I have had to massage the daily grind out of my daughter and energise her and two of my lady friends is beyond count lol.

The overall method: Massage the whole body with a firm, but aware approach, reducing massage pressure where even this level of massage generates intense pain. Make a note of where the pain is and the intensity level. Would suggest no more than two massages per week along with the monitoring of pain intensity, either increases or decreases and muscle tension felt by the masseuse. Notate how the patient felt when working different muscle zones and what scenes or emotions played out.

Continue using this technique until a marked reduction in pain by receiver and muscle relaxation tension measured by the provider happens. This level is the point I call stability, and it is the jumping off point for more in-depth introspection of both body and mind.

Although I can use my intuition even when this muscle tension is causing aggravated pain, the amount of effort is much more strenuous when they are in this state. It is also more advantageous to destress the person before adding stress by remembering their past trauma.

The pinpoint pain spot technique: The patient has now relaxed markedly, and we can continue with a firmer massage on the pain spots found previously. I used acupressure, trigger point massage etc. When applying a slowly firmer pressure to the pain spot area you need to get your client, patient to breathe deeply and with eyes closed, have them describe any feelings that come up while you are working there. Nb. The recording of symptoms can also happen in the overall body massage method. It worked for me when I was having a gentle Bowen therapy massage, but only, mild memories occasionally and more so when I was getting electronic acupuncture from two accredited practitioners.

Water intake will need to increase to flush out the toxins released from muscles and organs both after a massage and most especially should an emotional release occur while getting massaged. You may notice flu-like symptoms after this also. You don't have the flu just an allergic reaction from the flushing out of the emotion and related toxins.

Useful tools I have employed in muscle release therapy include the massaging vibrator. Use a reasonably robust model with variable speed. The electronic acupuncture needle. Have made entire sections of my neck and face convulse with this. It also can feel as if you are driving a red-hot needle into yourself so go slowly, as unless you can take the pain there is little gain. The spa and float tank was useful for its vibration, and it's warm womb emotional resemblance although the first time I used it, it upset my stomach and I chucked. Bad birth?

A lot of the books, I read refer to one's search for self-realisation, in other words, mental health, symbolically as peeling the onion. The symbolic onion, us has two focuses and two ways of being peeled lol.

The first method is through the body's musculature. Went to an old male Chinese acupuncturist for acupuncture. He looked at me disdainfully and shook his head. He said something along the lines "that acupuncture can let loose your bad emotions", and for this reason, he'd treat me with Chinese herbs. So acupuncture can pinpoint where the body's blockages are and like the old Chinese Master's who saw them so can we too as attuned empaths, as discolourations on the body. Or, you can just use the electronic acupuncture tool mentioned previously and run it over your whole body along the lines of Chi flow and record where it beeps.

The pain intensity levels are either, a sharp red-hot searing needle, a moderate, significant area flexing and on one occasion I had loss of body function, knees buckling until the falling stopped the current, a minor muscle vibration to nothing, the last two equating to average.

Although this method reduces reaction to electronic stimuli back to normal, I find that it is temporary and usage symptoms do return with less severity sometime later as the world intrudes or deeper levels of the musculature become exposed.

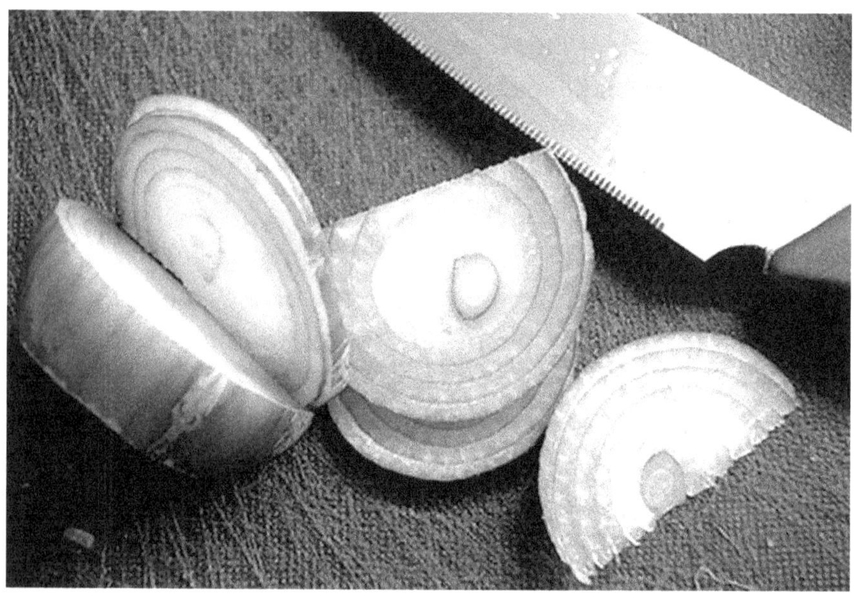

Following on from the first method, you can utilise a massage technique called Rolfing, once upon a time an extremely painful, intense massage. It equates to the acupressure point or aura discolouration mentioned above. Read that Rolfing has mellowed in today's environment.

Rolfing was in its inception extremely painful; intense massage of the primal emotion locked muscles. Way too harsh and in your face if you hit a primal emotional blockage for anyone suffering depression. It would be like running into a brick wall fast and just as injurious emotionally as well as physically if released. It would also be too painful for anyone already tenderised by the current emotional instability.

During the current treatment, Rolfing or any other massage style we should try to get the patient to recognise the pain as an emotion or emotional scene in their heads, eyes closed. During acupressure or electronic acupuncture, you can see images both from this life and others especially if you and the practitioner had previous life encounters as I did with the Bowen masseuse.

The problems with just physical massage and acupuncture remedial action are that firstly it's hit and miss, very dependant on the practitioner's skills at degree and seeing and correcting problems arising during the session. Secondly, it can promote a full-blown memory of the event when performed too forcefully or by the wrong sex, as the sex of the originating offender magnifies the reaction. This happening at a point in your existence where you aren't ready to remember it is both detrimental and sometimes mind-blowing.

Kriyas

Kriyas are muscular contractions that we have when we are close to revealing our inner fears, hates, i.e. primal emotional blockages. It is the body's way of releasing the trauma of the original event from the muscle involved. It is also the body's way of stopping the initial shock being accessed too early in our recovery.

Kriyas are natural body movements and self-repair, and as such are in no way associated with epilepsy as they only surface when we get close to the initial event in deep meditation, or sometimes after coming out of sleep, as experienced by myself, and can be stopped consciously, whereas epilepsy cannot.

Some of my Kriya's relate to my eyesight, tremors around the left eye pertaining to my post-birth 3rd eye trauma shutdown. Left cheek being pulled back to make me watch something I didn't want to see, In early childhood. My stomach (fear and rage) contractions I believe this relates to two nuns in preschool and detention after school, with possibly being locked in a closet. I experience horrible claustrophobic feelings at times nowadays, now that I am getting close to the memory, sometimes leading into full constrictive, shrinking into a foetal position. Never had these severe claustrophobic reactions ever previously in my life, other than when it first happened.

I am aware of and can break the muscle contraction cycle at any time and if it occurs to you know that you can also.

The first picture is one of me in peaceful meditation.

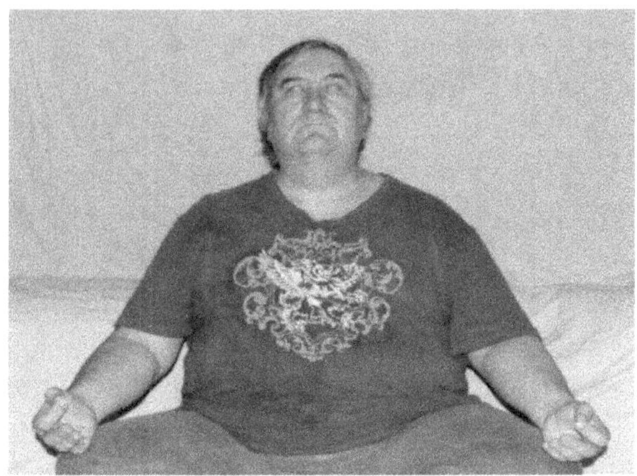

The second photo is where muscle spasms in the stomach region have contracted for a few minutes and have altogether broken the tranquillity and body posture.

The term Kriya comes from the yoga-practising religions and philosophies and have been known about for thousands of years as emotional trauma release effects.

Chapter 2
The Mental: Inside your head, Therapies

Spirit animals or anima in western terminology

I'll start the explanation using western jargon firstly. The brain is divided into many parts, several of which relate to the time when man didn't think he just reacted, this being the animal brain, anima. This reactive brain also has many levels, animal and reptilian being two.

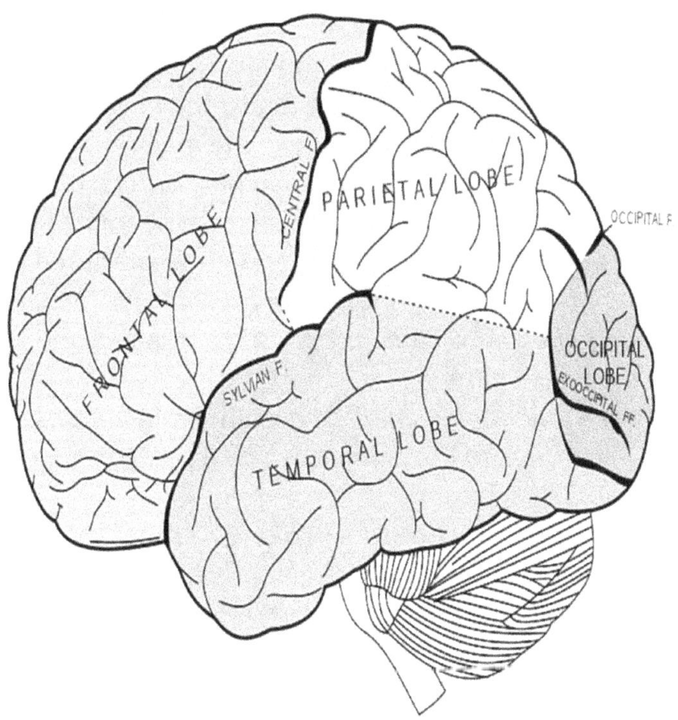

Being a cognitive race humanity now underutilises or actively hides the animal part of their mind in their day to day affairs. It is especially true for people with mental problems. Because we have become civilised and thoughtful, we have in most cases lost contact with this part of ourselves.

A lot of our emotional responses come from this part of our brain, the automatic fear, flight response being the much-used example. However, the animal mind plays a much more significant role in our lives than we can imagine. It influences our ability to touch and interact with each other.

So cutting off ourselves from our animal self also separates us from each other. Something that Western man has done exceptionally well, both refusing to acknowledge this or do something about reconnecting with themselves.

The American Indians recognised that one could bury the animal in man at his peril because it turns a group, tribe or pack animal into a single, lonely being. So they instead of hiding the beast sought to understand that part of themselves better and in doing so grew both as a being and as a group.

I was an accountant on an Aboriginal centre for three months and broached the subject with the leader because we were involved in a battle between right, (finding past monetary and asset losses) and majority rules. He seemed to understand what I meant by spirit animal to help him in his battle. Unfortunately, the majority ruled, and I in a full tribal council meeting got given my marching orders, he resigned, and I couldn't follow up on that brief discussion. Spirit animals could very well be a part of all tribal cultures even in today's westernised environment.

"Jung talks of the anama:" In Jungian psychology: The unconscious or true inner self of an individual, as opposed to the persona, or outer aspect of the personality.

The feminine inner personality, as present in the unconscious of the male. It is in contrast to the animus, which represents masculine characteristics."

"Cosmides and Tooby also state in a brief "primer" on their website,[6], that "...the brain is a physical system. It functions like a computer," "...the brain's function is to process information," "different neural circuits are specialized for solving different adaptive problems," and "our modern skulls house a stone age mind."

I have no dispute with the Western sciences attempts above to explain mind and the way we interact based upon chronological, mental segregation of data in the latter, or the fact that we have an inner self that has both masculine and feminine characteristics.

Back to the animal mind and the American Indians way to re-contact it. One goes and performs a looks within journey (a meditation to quieten the mind and then a visualisation). Someone is reminding me that you should do the symbolic, Aborigine and American Indian traditional act of cleansing with a smudge stick or incense, just waving the smoke over and around you (symbolic magic). A similar easy to use method take a shower and see all the muck washing off you.

You then retire to your retreat or a quiet, darkened room, meditate and then perform a creative visualisation: forest setting or sea, whatever one is drawn to use. During the session, you see an animal, bird, fish, or even insect that makes its presence felt in your mind.

Once you know what it is, then it's time to get acquainted with it and ask for an action it symbolises to help you and your animal mind to get better attuned and acquainted with each other.

Once shown the action, perform it, best alone as some of the activities in a group or publicly can draw ridicule and this is something that would discourage many from completing it.

As mentioned previously, the animal's movement will engender an energy flow within you. Animal spirit or animal portion of our brain?

The Eagle was my first animal spirit followed by the bear for a long, long time.

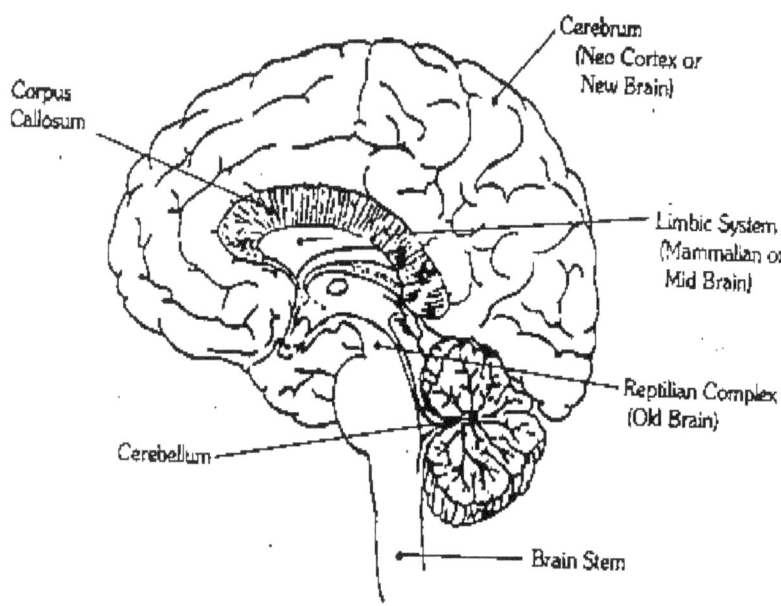

The choice is yours whatever one calls it.

The photo above is how I blow an animal spirit into another person. You visualise, intuit the animal that best suits your patients needs then bring up the palm close to the lips and blow the spirit into the person.

The distance of recipient is no barrier to the transmission as I have performed this many times with Sxxxx in Melbourne and me in Adelaide and had good short to medium-term results.

The purpose and result of doing so is to assist in the awakening of that part of their being, temporarily fortifying them with that emotional quality. The only drawback is that spirit transfers are only temporary unless you follow up with the previously mentioned exercises. And so because Sxxxx just accepted the temporary help, she fell back into negativity quickly, usually one to two weeks. Multiple remedial uses showed no loss of efficacy.

Remember these animal spirits shown are representational of where you are and the emotional quality you require improving. Just as a mirror is a sight of you physically so too are these a view of your internal emotional needs and direction. Each animal has a different primary characteristic.

Creative visualisation versus Looks within Journeys

Creative visualisations are guided introspective, imaginary journeys; eyes closed, usually, in the dark. The constraints can be whatever the group leader tells you to follow. Some of the ones I felt useful are:

Individual:

1 Searching for the light: That is everyone has a particularly beneficial colour that they should attract to them to assist or heal, during the eyes

closed introspection. They seek out that colour until it is the only thing there is and then just bathe in it until you've had enough. Each colour is representative of an emotion. So what you are doing here is enhancing the positive or suppressing the harmful feeling and this way you support yourself.

2 Envision yourself in the middle of a forest and seek out whatever is there that you need. It can be a feeling or an object which in turn creates an effect or a spirit animal saying Hi and seeking you to bond.

3 Envision yourself in the ocean: Here there are many things to look at; the ocean depth gives one an indication of where they are on the journey. The ocean beings whether they are friendly or frightening to just, the peaceful sensation of floating and swimming.

4 Using a crystal: project yourself into it and search the catacombs within it. So many doors to open and seek your answers to there. The inward crystal journey is where I received my colour healing so if you require healing choose the right door for you in the maze within the crystal. Each entry holds a secret applicable to you. "Seek, and ye shall find. Knock, and the door will be opened for you." As the Bible quote says.

Group:

All of the above instead of doing it on your own you search for the others and then journey together.

Looks within journeys are merely the same as the above introspective journeys within yourself, only this time one looks at where you are leading.

My own:

Many times I have used a frog guide to look into the pond of myself. Worked quite well for a while but like all things fades with overuse. Thinking back the frog may have been my spirit animal at the time so if a water animal or fish appears, use it to delve into your emotional blockages.

You do not have to go on retreat or go on solitary vision quests to be able to use the above techniques usefully. All you have to do is remember that practice makes one better and only follow the guide until the journey within takes you elsewhere, a different animal or living being.

Symbolic Magic

The above is the visualisation required, one of pouring sand over a person or yourself. The picture below is the locations I used while healing and calming Sxxxx. Many times I aided in getting her to sleep better, while both close and when interstate. When necessary I used this technique as a calmative, emotional stabiliser and occasionally as a pain deadener.

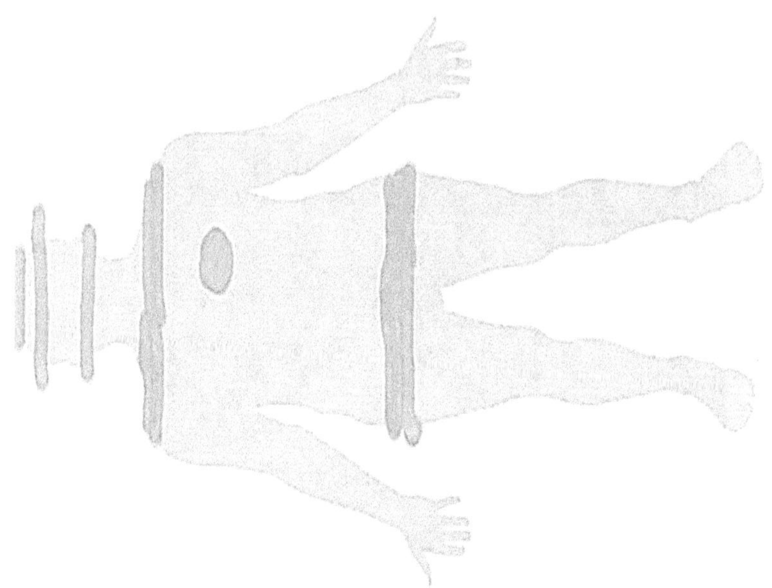

She reported excellent results regards sleep, moderate regards calming and small re pain reduction.

Rebirthing

Breathwork: while rhythmically drumming and deep breathing one can also trigger a similar response. The rebirther that chased my spirit out of my body was drumming. Lol, a reaction in the extreme.

Most of the time it should only bring up minor emotional hiccups and as I was told by the practitioner, stale air because at the time I was entirely expelling all my lung capacity, air that hadn't released for a while. So it had engaged the fear-flight response with enhanced breathing.

The Shower Cleansing

While taking a shower close your eyes and envision all this greenish muck that's sticking to you being washed away down the drain. It's amazing how much more refreshed one is after doing this. Was one of the techniques used on Sxxxx, especially in long-distance healing and she did use it frequently.

Chapter 3
Meditation

Why would I recommend meditation as a therapeutic method for depression? The purpose of meditation is to primarily quieten the racing mind and bring stillness and peace, a state beneficial for everyone. The second purpose that meditation has is the opening up of areas within the memory. This method is the second process in peeling the onion, memories which we had purposefully hidden due to them being too disturbing to be remembered safely when they occurred. Unfortunately, this releasing does take some time to achieve, but the former a quiet mind is relatively easily mastered in a short space of time.

The first purpose and description I can give is meditation is any activity that lessens the mind's endless chatter and control and allows one just to experience the total me effect emotionlessly rather than controlling it. To become a reactive, attentive, undisturbed concentrated mind rather than the scatterbrain, one starts out as.

The different methods I feel will be useful are in order discovered are: (2nd): Mantra or specific word repetition as a focus to stop the mind's constant chatter and idle imaginings. When I first started, I would mentally begin repeating Han So (Hindu mantra) eyes closed semi-lotus position. Then after a while, I got bored, and images would take over, then, would get back into the repetition, etc. After the 1st week of around a half hour or so of constant mental not verbal repetition per night, I was remaining in the repetitive mode throughout, feeling very focused and quiet regards other thoughts.

Watched a Sufi Turkish series Younis Emre and because of his constant repetition throughout the day, he became enlightened. Now I'm not suggesting anyone with emotional issues requiring treatment do this for that purpose. Your purpose is to get your mind away from harping on your worries which Sxxxx did regularly and instead, replacing them with this constant repetition.

Have never been overly religious and saying I am God didn't do anything for me back then. Have never tried since, as other specific rather than sacred guiding mantras are being provided daily now.

Did vocally chant group Om and Om Mani Padme Hum repeats but these didn't do anything to or for me. No energy flowed so no effect.

Saying I am God or the reverse could be useful for some people's conditions.

Does your mantra have to be given to you by a guru or have a religious flavour? Probably not although I will admit that specific mantras would probably induce a vibratory frequency or belief more attuned with and beneficial to conditioning the mind than others.

Finding an empathic guru that would know the difference may, however, be difficult if not impossible in today's physically oriented world.

If one perseveres with the mantra until one achieves total concentration it works, but remember the mantra is a crutch and at some stage, you will like me release it.

(1st & current method) The Buddhist Monkey Mind technique: just let your thoughts and imaginings play on the back of one's eyes when closed. Best done in the dark as light does shine through my eyelids, and it becomes the focus. Although it is quite impressive exploring the different shades of colour eyes closed, especially in the sunshine as I move my head, almost like watching a partial spectrum of the rainbow, depending on what light source you are using, however, it is a distraction.

Breathe slowly and regularly and watch what plays like a movie in your mind, neither desiring nor rejecting what the mind is churning out.

This technique was very time-consuming, and it took some time to re-attain the quietness of tranquillity in this meditation as compared to the concentration overload action that the repetition method achieved, but couldn't be repeated.

For a variety of reasons the main one being that it can be performed before going to sleep without the interaction or disturbance of others, I have continued with it to this day.

It is a useful gauge as to what is troubling one without being overwhelmed by the thoughts. It's almost like a conscious dream state and while in that state one can quite easily slip into sleep while doing this as well as after on finishing the meditation. I, purposefully meditate in a lotus position so as not to fall asleep, however. Although because I have increased the time spent, I do regularly slip into REM dream state lately while meditating. Also on occasion, I commence dreaming while still awake recently.

At best have dropped off seconds after my head hits the pillow. On a few occasions per year, it can induce a wide-awake state that, unfortunately, this will require a second session to deactivate the wide-awake racing mind. As sleep problems were part and parcel of Sxxxx's depressed's life, it would have been beneficial, but I couldn't get her to keep doing it, even though she realised the benefits and on many occasions said she should and would.

I believe that the Tai Chi movements and the concentration of that body motion, flowing technique might eventually produce a similar but more in line with a not mind-blowing experience effect.

The 180-degree full seeing: that is allowing the eyes to see all visual sensory data that is in the entire range of the eyes sight, without giving any specific item our attention. This unfocusing produces a sensory overload within the mind.

It is incredible that we can see everything in front and to the sides, all around and yet restrict ourselves to just items of interest, desire, and importance. It's unfortunate that we need to concentrate to remove our blinkers and allow this to happen so, on the whole, I don't practice this method often.

(7)" The posture of zazen is seated, with folded legs and hands, and an erect but settled spine. The hands are folded together into a simple mudra over the belly. In many practices, the practitioner breathes from the hara (the centre of gravity in the belly), and the eyelids are half-lowered, the eyes being neither fully open nor shut so that the practitioner is neither distracted by nor turning away from external stimuli."

I have purposefully omitted other meditation styles as they can be too disruptive.

I got talked into changing mine and attempting the Zazen meditation style recently. However, if you have been like me, a particular style user then performing other techniques then changing can induce or begin to cause a superconscious event. It almost made me vomit and have a queasy stomach for the rest of the day as well as commencing the eye and 3rd eye flutter superconscious prelude.

Changing meditation styles can trick the mind into superconscious events so be careful.

The difference between my meditation and this is that one can assess where one is in their mental stillness, and I find the visions useful, not distracting. Also, my method doesn't chain one into a fixed routine for life.

It was interesting to note in my pictures of me meditating and then having it broken by kriyas that only after a few minutes of meditation my eyes had already started looking upwards. A meditation effect that I had entirely not noticed while preparing for the photo. I suppose I concentrated on meditating, or my body naturally assumes this level quickly now.

Don't forget to wear casual clothing as it lessens any bodily discomfort and find a position that is for you balanced. For me, the crossing of my legs in the opposite manner to that in the photo disturbed rather than enhanced the meditation when I tried it once and, therefore, was a position, not in balance when I tried changing it.

Experiment with the meditative position until it feels right for you.

Your body posture changes as muscles relax, there will be increased digestive sounds and erect posture and skeletal alignment. These physical body changes happen automatically as your meditation gets more profound, so, neck clicks and cracking elsewhere, shoulders for me, isn't uncommon. The muscles will also start relaxing markedly. Remember that meditation is a whole you affect not only your mind. Stomach noises will also increase, and this is a natural body function effect.

Some of the physical manifestations as one goes deeper and deeper into oneself; lotus position are in the order that I have felt them. For a man, one's balls seem to drop physically at a certain initial, mental, depth level of meditation and at every time one gets to that level again.

The next level was just to feel mentally contented and at peace and this lasted for a long time.

The meditative state encourages the flow of energy at various times during the meditation. When it initially hits the brain, it produced some warm, pleasurable feelings and sights like fireworks going off within my mind, with the smile of satisfaction easily discernible. However as with all things pain followed this pleasure.

The next level many years after commencing this was that my eyeballs would unconsciously rotate upwards so that when my eyelids were exposed, they just showed white eyeballs. Seeing this perturbed and frightened Jo in our close Spiritualist circle.

The eyeball rotation **is not** a forced motion; it happens naturally when that level happens. Copying this is merely ego controlling and harmful to meditation stability.

Rapid eye movement just after the eyes turn upwards at this stage of meditation can predict an awakening or superconscious experience about to happen. It is especially true when the 3rd eye starts also blinking after our eyeballs begin rapidly moving sideways. Remember just let the meditation follow its path and just, experience it, don't control it.

This level of contentedness can last for many years. Remember this is all in your head, the conscious mind.

The next level, where I am at, is when one's locked muscles start to relax, that is muscles that have been in lockdown (constant on, off transition) commence to relax. When you get them relaxed, your body tends to straighten up of its own volition without being whacked into it as one Zen tradition does, and one's breathing becomes yogic at times with the ensuing flows of energy.

Another effect as you unlock more and more of your body is that as your muscles relax you may feel a certain amount of pain. i.e. just recently after coming out of meditation found my left side jaw hurt. As I had been holding my lower jaw in and read this showed an introverted persona many years ago, the pain hopefully indicates signs of jaw realignment.

When one begins assimilating the body back into the total you the waves of energy increase from a stream to a roar during meditation and the total you is affected. Accept this as part of the whole process and keep meditating. Also, when the passage of energy increases to this level it is no longer a nuisance and hindrance to the meditative state but part of it.

Mudra can be incorporated into one's meditation as many statues of the Buddha and Bodhisattvas show. Be aware however that imitating some mudras without being in tune with yourself is either useless at best or can induce incorrect flows of energy to your detriment.

Mudra

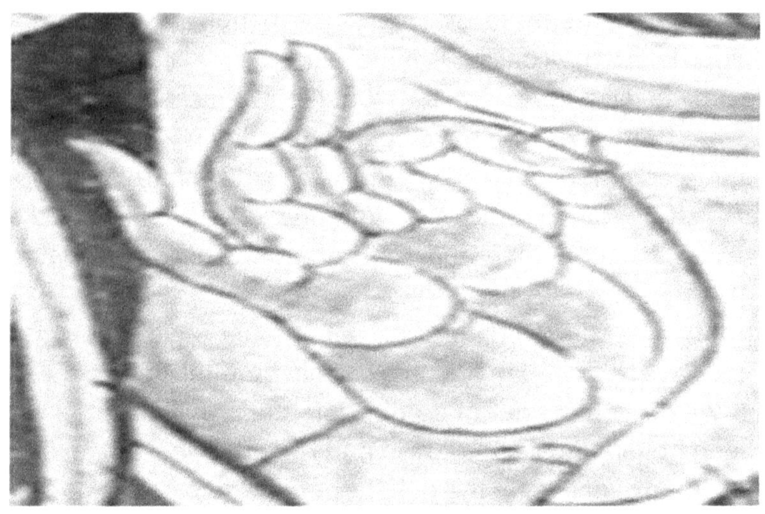

Bodhidharma with the Vitarka (Gyana) mudra

Remember that each mudra is specific in opening the pathways energy channels within. So start and stay with the usual Vitarka (Gyana) hand one above and the crossed legs, semi or lotus position as I find it assists in achieving balance and calm.

Semi lotus, as one gets older, is excellent, even a chair with both feet planted firmly on the ground, although on a chair palms resting just above the knees is a good energising one. Just checking the Vitarka (Gyana) mudra is open while the palms on legs is closed, so try it out, occasionally alternate. Body positioning is different from mudra, finger energy channel change which can be more disorienting.

Another Buddha statue mudra for me was discordant back when I tried it but then automatically assumed the position temporarily one morning when I hit a new level in my meditation. Your body will assume the position when it is needed.

The Vitarka (Gyana) still feels right, but it is a calming mudra while the other is an active one and while you may occasionally change for short periods to readjust yourself I found I kept returning to it consistently with very short breaks when not.

As shown above, there are passive internal affecting and active external effecting mudras or open and closed ones.

Rehash

Part of the meditation journey is finding a balance so cease meditation if you become disturbed by as in my case the pins and needles Kundalini channel blockage imbalance. Merge back into today's physical reality until you have by occasionally testing achieved no pain or negative sensations while meditating. It is especially true after coming across deep-seated mental and muscle blockages. Don't overdo it!

A couple of last pointers: the first being as my brain injury psychologist told me "You will heal in a plateau ascension climb towards health." Well, meditation is the reverse one descends into oneself, and admittedly some of the plateaus in meditation take a long time to cross till the next level is reached.

Never fall into the trap that you have reached the bottom of yourself and don't think you'll always feel better after meditating. I am now regularly coming out feeling the exposed muscular soreness of a lifetime.

So meditation has cycles of awareness, firstly just mental, then as one taps into one's self-awareness of the total you both mind and body align.

I allow my meditation to flow whatever is required through to me whether it be energy, mantras, self-instruction, and conditioning or the thoughtless state, something zazen and its teachers don't allow. I recently compared Zazen to the bird in the cage. Indeed, it is safe but can the bird ever fly free if caged too long? My experiences of the comments received by Zazen practitioners suggest no.

Always, just experience the meditation as it happens. Actively controlling it is not meditation. However, total concentration does also snap one into alternative mental states, and this can occur more often as we reach the deeper stages of meditation. It is a good starting point.

Also be aware that as one moves up the chakras and becomes more in tune with oneself that just getting near as I do when I start seeing this globe of light (3rd eye vision) in my forehead you will begin to shake rattle and roll as your muscles try to release the locked down musculature.

A bit more on chakras becoming aware of them is more progress of least resistance within the chakra rather than an ascension vertically up the body. In my case contact has been rare with all except 3rd eye and above.

The semi Lotus cross-legged pose with thumb and 1st finger clasped with the other three fingers outstretched resting on my knees in a mudra position I have found to be useful and calming in both the Mantra and Monkey Mind meditations.

Repetition is tedious, so I suggest internal meditation styles morning and night, before sleep for 15 to 30 minutes or as long as your feet can stand it and physical activity several times a day to promote body health and if you join a Tai Chi group social interaction or join a group and activity you like.

The Visions

Lastly, a lot of the ideas and past lives, and this lifetime memory experience awakening that are in the book The Bio-electric, Prana, Kundalini, Reiki, Chi, Sha Man's Shaman Ways came to me after meditating. I suspect it is a mirror of the way The Corpus Hermeticum. *"The first book involves a discussion between Poimandres (also known as Nous and God) and Hermes, supposedly resulting from a meditative state, and is the first time that Hermes is in contact with God. Poimandres teaches the secrets of the Universe to Herme"* got written.

I do not believe I can make that assertion and would think that Hermes meditative states would have been similar to mine. At best it was influenced by another spirit rather than God, but as we get into deep meditation, it is not unreasonable to assume we can reach into the collective originating mind.

Christmas 2013 and dad finally got me to remember he was one of the causes of me turning off my spiritual sight due his locked in pain from the war.

Lots of other visions some listed below, but that is my story, and you need to proceed with yours.

Personal effects of meditation

The meditation session got me to around stomach reintegration of body mind and for the first time disassociated me from the world in a sort of tranquil cocoon for several days.

Physical events that trigger hidden memories will allow you to access more of yourself. So be aware that the effects of one's meditation can produce results that can last past the meditative state. Be conscious of the outcome, enjoy the tranquillity, separation or whatever and know it will pass.

Lastly, something that I have recently found out is one needs to change as one's meditation changes and what was once a distraction, e.g. energy flow is now just a part of the whole meditation process.

This is true, even though now what was once a trickle is a roar in energy flow. Now that I have stilled the mind, it courses through the whole of my body and not just parts or the backbone as it did once.

Also, be aware that visions including past life memories will surface as you go deeper and deeper into yourself.

One morning was all over the place, partially due to overly sleeping in, and the initial phase of the meditation was all about left side and right side eye balancing.

Once balance was getting to completion and body was straightening up was thrown back in time with a vision of the wagon train memory only this being after the event when I realised who I had hurt.

It set off a massive denial memory, and then the phone rang breaking the vision and showed me why I feel so responsible for Sxxxx. Might also explain why I have tried to save her from herself so passionately in this lifetime.

Meditation had this immense third eye representation giving me a pressure pain headache when I focused on it. It was the closest I have come to opening it and releasing the muscular constrictions I have placed to stop myself from seeing honestly again.

Meditations since have been unbalanced again, so brushes against one's primal fears reverse some of the order and balance achieved previously or perhaps open up some of that hidden which now needs reintegration to make it balanced again.

The peaceful darkness is full of nuances, of dark and light. Colours, when seen in meditation, are still causing facial, neck and stomach Kriyas contractions. Last few meditation sessions have produced almost total bursts of energy over all my body as well as an awareness of the whole me rather than just a mental recognition of the just mind state.

Meditation again thrust at me the best 3rd eye visualisation to date and looking remarkably like a huge eye with reflections, images in it. Still very disturbed meditations for several days after this.

Strange vision last night with Star of David, Sat-Kona being the most applicable explanation mixed with a compass background and some young robed woman with a flower garland on her head resembling a Tarot card.

The night after again Star of David, although the Hindu version is more applicable to the meditative state.

"In the oldest known Vedic literature, Sri Brahma-Samhita [in that it has been attributed to Lord Brahma and composed shortly after creation], the Sat-Kona is mentioned in a description of the supreme abode of Goloka, the abode of Krsna." Although what the sprinkles of light around the inner edges of the star are unknown other than a sudden jolt of energy was felt while I saw the star, so possibly Kundalini.

"The Masonic compasses symbolize an implement of virtue by which we are taught to circumscribe (create a boundary around) our passions and keep our desires within due bounds." It is unknown whether this relates to my finding the boundaries of my desires, seeing the pentacle twice and this once has undoubtedly suppressed my appetite since.

Meditation suppressed the sexual desire for almost two months. Then went from that described above a medley of physical shakes, energy flows and quiet from one night to what felt an expansion of the area within myself and total disruption of the peaceful state previously accessed. If this is a spiritual awakening, it is indeed not what I was expecting, but, just goes to show that the actual is more often than not what one expects.

It seems the 3rd eye fears and apprehensions have passed as the visual equivalent no longer causes physical shakes when I see it, and the vision is now inside my head.

Further images of the 3rd eye have me realising that it is both an awakening of my pineal gland, but it can see in both directions both externally and internally as an indicator of where I am.

Now onto the next primal: the rage against what happened in childhood now that the mind is stilling again in meditation.

Again starting to see the distant aura around visions when coming out of sleep. Body is catching up to the mental awakening but slowly. The colours have become more softer pastels than normal bright ones

Also, the images of Buddha have been replaced with Shiva firstly and now blurry pictures of several people. My thoughts now aren't muffled as if received through barriers. They are direct and loud and seem to originate in the centre of my mind.

Remember that like the colourful Star of David we all have bits and pieces of the puzzle we have made ourselves strewn across our lifetime. Our journey is to find and open them.

Choose the meditation style you find most useful and be careful when changing from one form to another.

Chapter 4
The Bio-electric energy

Why do I include the bodies own bio-electricity as a method of finding release from one's troubles? It has more to do with the path I am on than my experience with Sxxxx. Although I broached this and the meditation subjects with her, she was loath to take up these methods. She was quite happy to take my psychic healing, but not generate her own. I have found that energy flow aids in my release of past trauma. The energy has quite often concentrated on the areas burdened by locked muscles and has been the precursor of release. The East calls this energy Kundalini.

Interesting the photo is suggesting that the serpent Kundalini rises more readily during meditation. Lots of different things happen in meditation, and the purpose is just to experience them and not be further influenced by them once they have occurred. In another painting of the Buddha unsure if the lotus symbolises our base chakra that I saw at the beginning of my spiritual journey. The Lotus the Buddha is sitting on looks very similar to our base chakra, although what I saw looked more like flames than a flower and as flames are more energy-related, I would go with my vision.

During your meditation flows of energy will occur. When it initially hits your brain enjoyable feelings arise, but this passes with time and can be followed by feelings of pain as previously mentioned.

Flows will also occur during Tai Chi or Qui Gong meditation or exercises.

Chapter 5
Beware Of and Be Aware Of section

Primal Emotions

Remember you are made up of spirit and matter, and there are things the soul cannot and will not handle, and it can be frightened out of your body.

So if you have a nasty mental primal fear confrontation like I did during a rebirthing, and you see a frightened face flying away, and then you start feeling as if your batteries are getting flatter over the following days, talk yourself back.

Was about to see the sight or fear and off my contorted, fearful spirit shot and I watched it rise and fade from view, hence stopping the rebirthing.The rebirthing practitioner also thought something had happened and likewise stopped. Any extreme fear experience can induce the same flight scenario, so if people go into coma's or seem to be fading after such a current traumatic event or reliving a past experience, an attempt to talk them back could work wonders.

The physical side effects, of getting close to one's primal emotions, are involuntary muscle spasms. The worse the hidden emotion is; the more significant the muscular contractions that occur and the more of the body that is involved.

Primal emotions get locked into specific muscles and organs depending on the type, and there they become permanently secured. That is the affected muscle locks and unlocks so quickly as not to be noticeable other than as a fire or ice sensation in the muscle when one overuses it. Very noticeable in old age.

Knew of my frozen leg muscle many years ago but it's only just in the last few years it's developed an icy cold or sometimes boiling feeling.

The involuntary spasms can affect the whole body, and one can shake on one's bed when triggered in meditation, rebirthing or waking from the dream state. You spasm into a tight muscle pulsing, eventually over a minute contracting into the foetal position.

Or they can be specific muscle-related, e.g. stomach muscles relating to fear, left, and now right eye twitches about sights in the past, not wanting to be released and remembered.

This shaking is the body's way of trying to release the emotion locked in that muscle.

I must say the more in-depth the meditation, the higher the chances are of you coming into contact with one of your demons. The scariest demons one will ever face are those which we have inside ourselves as we have been cultivating them for lifetimes.

If you go into a full foetal position, i.e.constrictive spasms multiple times each one crunching you up more, until one adopts a foetal position. It's getting intense physically and doesn't seem to be subsiding, just remember you are in control of the event and can break into normality at any time you wish.

Don't attempt to ride the Kriya out if it overpowers you as the emotional shock and physical constrictions can be incredibly intense. Remember each time you have a Kriya, muscular spasm you are releasing part of that past event.

I mentioned the wrong Kundalini effect of feeling like a pincushion due it flowing up my cold channel. Fevers result from it flowing up the hot channel. Possibly hallucinations from rushing too much up the central one directly into the brain. So check the patient to see if they have severe tingling sensations along with any of the effects mentioned.

The snarling demon face is also that of the person fighting against their demons and not giving in when they come close during meditation. The demons are also symbolic of your traumatic events in your life which you have to remember and reintegrate using current understanding.

So you can have both the non-emotive muscle spasms and ditto but with full-blown mental emotions in your face reactions that are unquestionably the harder to work through.

One has to stop and wonder if the externalised demons in the religions are just the internalised demons we face within ourselves. Remember that they guard and prevent the unknowing you from entering the gates of the temple which symbolises you.

Although not the Kriya, I had hoped to show my photo related to my meditation being broken by my stomach muscles starting to spasm and mudra and meditative state balance loss.

Probably for the best thinking back as I wouldn't want to react on my photographer. The other would have been detrimental to her, possibly causing a sympathetic flashback as her trauma and mine of being made to watch nasty shit, may have similarities. Group rebirthing sessions have had flow-on effects with multiple people being affected by one person releasing also.

The other Kriya's being acted out at this time are where my face resembles where fingers get thrust into my cheek, and my head was pulled sideways and forced to look at something I didn't want to see.

The third one I look like a growling angry beast with fingers bent into a claw shape and angry or scared as hell. Angry enough to react wildly, which I may have done in my early childhood, at around 7-8 years old. Believe this was the locked in a closet punishment at school.

Spiritual Healing

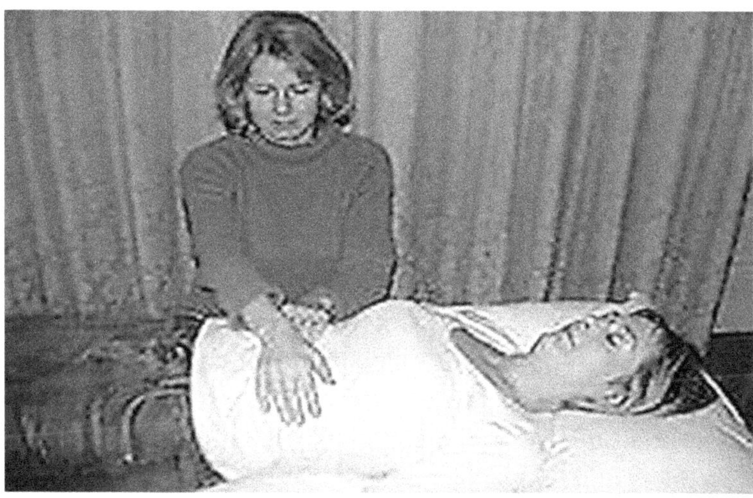

Went to an Intro to Reiki seminar and one of the ladies I healed just started crying when I used my spiritualist healing energy on her. She thanked me later as it had released something in her. One of my girlfriends lay down on my lap and my stroking her hair made her fall asleep, similar to what the old magnetic healers used to do.

In the spiritualist circles, I attended I used energy transference, Chi, psychic, Reiki or whatever one calls it for physical ailments and both it and visible light emanations for emotional issues. On occasion utilised sounds for the recipient to remember the past.

Something people can do is the simple sweep, i.e. sweeping the palm from the middle of the body to the nearest exit point hand or feet. This action has both a symbolic mental assist and a release of attached low-level emotional refuse through this cleansing action.

The other position spiritual healers use is just placing the hands on peoples shoulders and allowing the healing to flow there.

Energy transfer can also increase the bodies flow and open up emotional blockages, though in the whole only minor releases were recorded by myself, with a few crying during the session. After the healing, I would mention anything I had seen during the healing or received from the recipient.

An attempt at trigger therapy even before I knew about the method. Overall responses were positive regards the healing and better than average concerning the messages

In my early days, only a few sessions into psychic healing in the 1970's watched a spiritual healing gone wrong. A young woman was getting healing, and a middle-aged member with years of experience was giving it to her when they both started to shake violently, similar to electrocution, and both were very distressed.

He couldn't break the contact, and it took several people to disconnect them at which time they were both afraid and drained but at least back to normal. Must say I was as stumped by the event then as it was only the 3rd or 4th time I was there as was everyone else, and I had not read about any such occurrence.

In hindsight, if that or things start going strange, disconnect the contact because there are positive and negative people and putting the two together can be disastrous if the memories coincide or the vibrations and timing are right.

Also, healing can trigger primal releases though it is rare that both would go into a Kriyas muscular spasm episode at the same time. That is unless they interacted with one another re a past life memory surfacing, or each triggered a primal emotion in the other.

Certainly, a possibility, given the two people in question. Although usually, healing flows healer to healed, there have been several occasions when I have received the healing that I flowed some back towards the healer, so see if you can tell which direction it's moving.

To the person being healed a warning if you ever feel you are being drained or frozen cease the healing process immediately as energy is going out of you into the healer. If you went there for healing because you are ill, you certainly don't need to lose the chi, warmth, and health.

My Polish lady friend found this out once when receiving healing and suffered feeling frozen for several weeks after. She like my daughter never listens to me to reenergize themselves, and so the feeling lasted way longer than it should have.

Lastly, although I have used external concentrators (crystals) and still require them occasionally, all my healing is done in silence and without foreign objects or words. The theatrics of yelling "praise the lord" and Hallelujah" or any other similar words is relying on a placebo religious effect.

Be aware shit can happen even during spiritual healing.

Zen, Shaman and Gestalt trigger therapy

Almost forgot this one! Words have power, and certain words and messages will raise an internal emote that is either an emotion or a muscular jerk. Remember the Zen master confusing his pupil when he cast his cloak down for a lady so she shouldn't dirty her shoes with mud. His comments many miles later "I left the lady behind a long time back. You are still carrying her!"

The Vulcan Mind Meld LOL

Just as an afterthought I did use this merging of minds once with Sxxxx, and we both went through a mental visualisation together inside her head. It would probably be difficult to achieve unless one has been very close to the patient previously.

Self Indications

I know that when I have come across my primals I would start shaking my head in a no gesture. Listen to yourself if you are visually expressing a negative and cease. Still shaking no rarely now but less vehemently than before.

The Closed eye exercises

The following method was used by me to rebalance myself due to a physical brain injury. However, I have been told to include it here as an emotional left-side, right-side brain balance assessment.

The photo I have used with the oval over the right eye displays how I perceived the distortion with the right distortion skewed to the left eye and the left needing a cognitive switching of vision to see normally. It seemed to indicate my two brain hemispheres were not talking to each other, and one side was being utilised to a higher degree than the other as per the visual distortion seen in eyes closed meditation. The injury was proven by both neuro psyche testing and CAT scan as one frontal lobe was more damaged than the other.

Would suggest this test to psychiatrists and psychologists as a test for their patients as a simple right side, left side, predominance brain pattern determinant and as an assessment of brain injuries. Was some 80+% right side brain oriented after the toxic injuries per the eyes closed visual perception.

The circle's eyes closed is the normal perspective

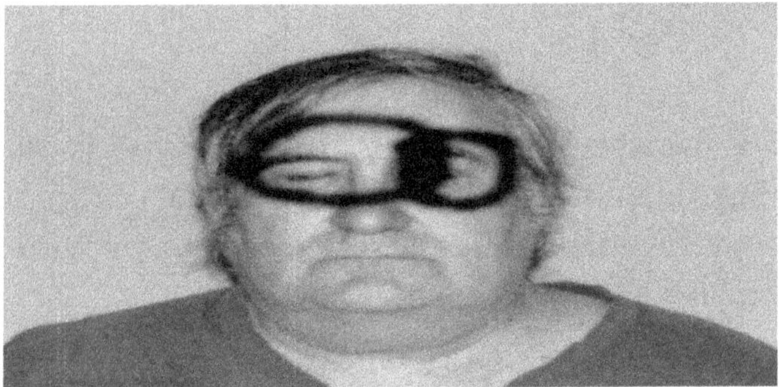

The perspective after my brain injury, eyes closed

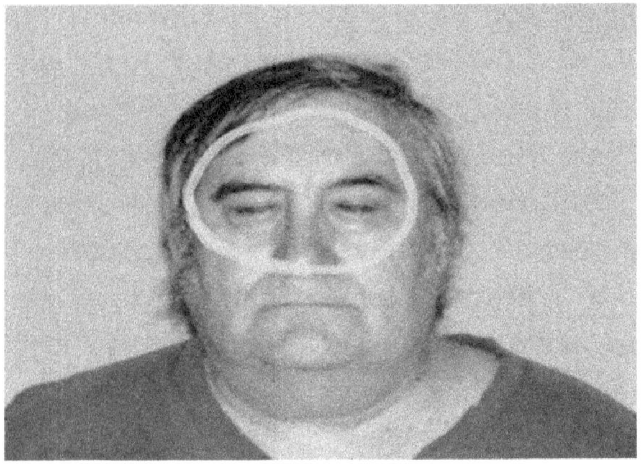

The perspective one gets in the initial meditation mental balance stage

Facial expressions

Recently, have noticed a lot of people with eyes when open being opened at different levels. This disparity when not a physical condition, I intuit can show an emotional imbalance. Now in some of the images, it also was intuited that this can indicate split personalities.

Other people when smiling seemed to be barring their teeth in anger, rather than smiling.

So facial observation may be indicatative of the emotional problems requiring attention.

Chapter 6
Psychologists, Psychiatrists

Regards psychologists and psychiatrists if I use Sxxxx's 30+ years of consultations as an indicator with a half dozen or so before her moving and another similar number interstate they are more like a herd of elephants. In the searching, they do more harm than good and although they have indicators to guide them several while I knew her made her worse, especially when she became dependant on them emotionally possibly transferring parental feelings and needs to them.

Two became frustrated and turned into antagonists against her rather than helpers. I had to spend a lot of time undoing what they did, even stopping her from injuring herself several times after her consultation with one diagnostic psychiatrist. It was especially true where they didn't comfort her and were pushy.

By the way, don't like her keep going ad infinitum to a psychologist and psychiatrist as the attachments you form with them exacerbates any rejection they show. She was heartbroken when one of her longtime female therapists had to let her go due to ill health.

She was even more betrayed and stirred by a male specialist and a female who was very unsympathetic. She may have just chosen the wrong ones, but after some ten odd consultants and some 34 years of visits, I really couldn't see any improvement.

Also, each one sooner or later ran out of analysis ideas, and it becomes just a social visit and you a cash cow if you go for more than a few months. Also, why pressure yourself with constant analysis? No-one is ever that bad or needy, have a break and see how you go before going back and if you don't perceive results or you start fighting with them, change.

During all of her 30+ years of consultations, all they could come up with was that she was Bi-polar. No-one saw the childish destructive alter ego that surfaced when she was going through awful emotional periods.

In fact, it was when this alter ego surfaced that she was and is exceptionally prone to suiciding. It took me weeks to submerge "the bitch" as I called her alter-ego brat and brought her normal personality back into the equation after her suicide attempts here. Although not entirely sure because what she showed the world usually was a fictitious personality, a lot of the time and it was difficult to pinpoint when she switched from normal to acting. After a lifetime of acting, it probably became difficult for her to know what was her and what was made up for others.

I had done an excellent job of burying her alter ego, but only just brushing the outer edges of the causes. As I mentioned due to a medley of both physical trauma, pain and work pressure, she succumbed again, and the bitch resurfaced. Although in a much quieter fashion and more as an aid that got her to seek help than the grave threat previously.

Psychologist, psychiatrist prodding of the indicators or telling someone what their problems are once they have seen the malaise during a session can be more like a surgeon going into an operation with a meat cleaver in one instance or a feather in another. Too heavy handed and for this reason endangering or too light handed and useless in the other.

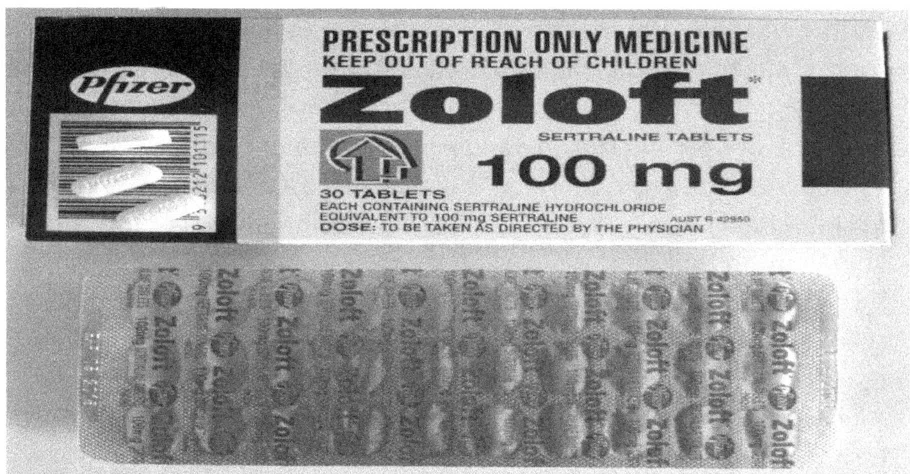

Remember that psychologists, psychiatrists are merely band-aiding the real cause of your problems with the drugs they prescribe to you.

Why do I say this? Because, after my minor brain injury the idiot I was under prescribed some of the shit for me. Yes, I was suffering from a brain injury with chronic fatigue symptoms, before taking the two medications, but after taking them, I was like at 10% capacity compared to what I had been previously and dumped them after a couple of days.

Chapter 7

My treatment of Sxxxx

Using a Gestalt, empathy method I the shaman merely told her what she was willing to show herself, and it was with this gentle approach that the onion got slowly peeled with the least harm. We were just beginning to access deeper memories when she decided to move interstate.

With Sxxxx, my intuition was accurate 90-95% re acupressure points and massage points and useful 60% of the time re emotional blockages and triggers. At other times(20%) I could see the strain prodding produced and let it go. The rest of the time entirely missed the mark or got no response, possibly meaning the emotion was too deeply buried.

The beginning: We met on a free relationship dating site, the purpose for me was to get some legal knowledge from her regards a work injury I had sustained. Well, the one-sided love affair blossomed, until I suspect it got too dangerous, hot to handle for her and she attempted her first suicide attempt. From there on it became a rescue mission, friendship for me, simply because she couldn't allow someone to get that close and I understood that fact.

The empathy or intuited facts were: something about a wall at her school surfaced several times. Her older brothers bullied her, with descriptions of their teasing growing in meanness and severity over several years. Her grandmother was only interested in male children and mistreated her, and her parents were cold.

It took quite some time to be able to receive anything from her initially as she had a barrier preventing both herself and me from accessing her problems. As I mentioned much of the time, she portrayed a fictitious outer appearance, and, acted this part excellently.

I spent at least half an hour each visit massaging her initially, two to three times per week. It is quite strange that I could pinpoint the trigger spots and go to them and in the initial finds made her jump in pain with little to moderate pressure. In conjunction with the message, I would use my psychic healing ability on both her body where I felt a disturbance and her head to calm her down.

Went to the beach one day and I got her to sit facing the waves and made wind sounds behind her trying to bring up the reason for her feeling lonely. Another beach visit with a friend of hers and had her build a sand castle and then beat the shit out of it to access the reason for her internal anger.

As mentioned when we had gotten her to a happy time, relaxed and enjoying life I began along with minor massages when necessary to work on her acupressure spots, and more in-depth empathic analysis regards her emotional repressions. We dredged up a grave concern that she had failed her daughters because of her depression taking control of her life. It took a lot of time to settle, but not overcome. More stuff regards her mother caring for others more than her.

Her second suicide attempt came with a phone call and me racing up to her house only to find the ambulance taking her away.

As with every attempt, she made it somehow disconnected the telepathic link I had forged with her, and it took some time to get the connection back to where it had been previously. By this time we had stabilised her sufficiently to have her working under a sympathetic and reasonable supervisor, and she for several months flourished in his department.

It was at this time she may have thought our relationship was reblossoming and told me she wanted to apply for a job in Melbourne so she could be with her daughters. I blew four animal spirits into her on the day of her interview, and she got the job.

Well, the job she had gone for was expecting a fully operational, tech-savvy employee, capable of just fitting in without any training and take the duties on running from day one.

She was good, but not a loner and without adequate support began falling apart, this being especially so after slipping over and hitting her head in the works carpark and having migraines later. Of course, she didn't report this and so, even after a call to her supervisor by me, who was very conciliatory Sxxxx finished working there.

I can tell you it is challenging to assist Adelaide to Melbourne and my only recourses were absent healing, that is sending energy healing long distance, using spirit animals for fortification and sleeping sand for better sleep. The problem with these methods is they are temporary, short to medium term fixes depending on the severity of her condition.

Before the end of our hundreds of phone help sessions here and hundreds more interstate, I had intuitively gotten the fact that she was afraid of her father, something she freely stated but was fearful of admitting. In fact, she had forgotten that she had mentioned him previously while discussing it. This dredging up of emotions indeed meant she was releasing them to me but did it force her away? I don't know?

One of Sxxxx's failures was that she expected me to do all the heavy lifting and saving. At best she meditated slightly.

It is important to mention that my involvement with the lady was 70% social 20% worker's Compensation case paperwork assist and 10% shaman treatment and this only showed marked improvement while she was in this state. All remedies once she left were attempts to stabilise at a distance and although some managed to do this for months at the beginning, the further she destabilised the shorter the treatments benefits lasted and the greater the frequency needed.

To put it plainly I probably treated her timewise less than her psychologists did, but she showed me more of herself in the couple of years than she had in over 30 years to the mental health experts she used.

The Checklist

General checklist.

Have them close their eyes and tell them to tell you the shape seen with eyes closed. If the eyes are distorted and not round with similar area, a right hand left-hand physical exercise routine should be attempted, along with concentrating on the weaker circle to reshape it. Once both eyes closed visions are balanced further work will need to be tried to make the two eyes a single being, you The physical exercise can be followed up with a creative visualisation of circles, eyes closed, and then alternately blinking to activate the lesser and recreate the one mind balance.

Have they ever been in an accident injuring their spine or neck? The answer does affect where and how hard you can massage.

When asleep do they remember their dreams and what colour are they?

Do they have sleep problems?

Do they have muscle tremors or pain and if so where?

Do they exhibit signs of Kundalini misdirection, goosebumps, prone to fevers or hallucinations?

Do they have shivery sensations over their body?

If so find how intense and how far up the spine the energy goes and the effect on the brain while flowing.

Do the pinch test on the shoulder to the neck area and notate if hard and degree of stiffness.

Again when performing a full body massage takes notes of areas requiring further attention.

Get them to describe what they think is the problem. Sometimes getting someone to talk about their perceived issues goes a long way to establishing trust and communication. Notate pertinent points, however, be aware that this is probably a smokescreen hiding the real issues. The other thing to check is that like the fisherman you'll sometimes catch a mullet when fishing for a marlin. However, this should not be overlooked as it shows progress and any release is better than no release.

Physical Healing checklist

Have a body outline chart and notate pain spots found and degree of pain felt by the patient when massaging.

If they are doing RH LH physical exercises, have them redo eye test weekly

Spiritual healing checklist

Run palm over the patient's body and notate where you feel energy fluctuations. These areas can indicate the type of emotion that is causing the blockage.

After the initial intuitive search, find and pinpoint the acupressure points and notate them.

Healing procedures

Start with a light massage or even a light massage with the electric vibrator.

If you are a spiritual healer Lay on hands, generally anywhere, and sweeps over the points found, to remedy blockages especially Kundalini overflows.

Continue with the above two until the stable, relaxed body state occurs.

Unless you are particularly skilfull, remain using the above.

A slight variation is add electronic acupuncture to the routine.

Bibliography

The fog picture on my cover: https://en.wikipedia.org/wiki/Fog#/media/File:Tree_in_field_during_ext reme_cold_with_frozen_fog.png

A lot of the material here was transferred from my book "The Bio-electric, Prana, Kundalini, Reiki, Chi, Sha Man's Shaman Ways."

The pictures of me also come from my book

Special thanks to Wikipedia for the pictures regards, the muscles, the cut onion, Shiva, Sat Kona, Masonic Triangle, Buddhist demon and human mind and brain.

The Zoloft photo: https://en.wiklpedia.org/wiki/Sertraline#/media/File:Zoloft_100_mg.jpg

Other publications by myself include:

The Bio-electric, Prana, Kundalini, Reiki, Chi, Sha Man's Shaman Ways

Cancer: The Proactive Spiritual Assist Method

UFO's and Spaceship Gods

Lament of a Paedophile Satanist's still surviving Ex-Wife. Compendium of three poems

God Sinned Greatly: Why Couldn't We Sin Slightly

Meditation: My Methods of Reintegrating Mind and Body

Contact: mahaete@gmail.com

Spiritual healing email: spiritualhealing@mahaete.com

Website Mahaete.com.

Revised 18/4/2018 corrections and significant inclusions.

FIT FOR SERVICE

John 10: 10 Says: "I have come that they may have life, and have it more abundantly." Life becomes living when Christ is first. Abundant living means you are in good condition or "fit" spiritually, physically, mentally and emotionally. That is what Fit for Service is all about. Fit for Service is a Christ centered health and wellness program that enables you to lead an abundant life the way God expects of a Christian.

As with any new program, the first step is to make the decision to do it. Nike is famous for the phrase "Just Do It". Those words are much easier said than done. However, with Fit for Service there are some basic commitments to focus on and incorporate into your daily living in order to become fit, more fit and the most fit you can be for service to the kingdom of God.

Your Fit for Service materials include a workbook, index cards for sharing recipes, and a prayer journal. The workbook will include the basics Fit for Service and topics for self study, helpful hints and articles. The prayer journal is to record your daily prayer time and Bible study. If you currently keep a prayer journal, please continue to use your journal and incorporate the thoughts and ideas for Fit for Service from your Bible study into the journal.

As stated before there are a few commitments necessary to ensure that you are successful in your journey to become fit for service.

1. Commitment
2. Prayer
3. Scripture Reading
4. Bible Study
5. Exercise
6. Live the life

A final commitment is to **"BE A PAL!"** No matter what is done in this life someone having a partner on the journey is better than going alone. So as embark on this journey to become the most fit to serve in God's kingdom **BE A PAL** to someone and bring them along. The basic course length is 6 weeks. Take this journey with a friend to encourage spiritual growth and gain a deeper relationship with God through being fit to provide services to His Kingdom.

FIT FOR SERVICE
1. COMMITMENT

When you commit to this program, you commit to faithfully reading the word, studying the scriptures to be spiritually and physically fit to provide services for His Kingdom.

2. PRAYER

Paul stated in Colossians 4:2 "Be devoted to prayer, keeping alert in it with thanksgiving." Prayer increases faith and improves spiritual practice. Fit for Service requires a commitment to pray every day and record your prayer in your prayer journal. Writing the prayer down provides an opportunity to focus on the request to God. Additionally, when the prayer is written you can look back and see how God has blessed you and answered your prayers. There are always opportunities to pray. Pray for your commitment to this program, pray for your family and friends and pray that you will not be tempted by food or any other issue to keep you from being healthy physically, spiritually, mentally and emotionally.

3. Scripture Reading

In 2Timothy 3: 16 -17: Every scripture is inspired by God and useful for teaching, for reproof, for correction, and for training in righteousness, 17 that the person dedicated to God may be capable and equipped for every good work. We are also commanded to study to show ourselves approved unto God. Studying God's word regularly and prayer are essential for every Christian. Regular reading of the Bible and prayer allows you to feed from God's word and will transform you spiritually and change your life. Discipline is the key. You must schedule the time to study and pray daily.

Those who study the Bible regularly know that studying the Bible requires a systematic approach. Your Fit for Service workbook includes a daily Bible reading guide. The guide was developed by Michael Coley. The guide divides the topics of the Bible into seven (7) topics that are covered on the same day of the week for year. Sunday's topic is the Epistles; Monday readings are from the Law and so on. Since studying the Bible is personal, the daily reading plan can be whatever you choose. The plan included in the workbook provides a tool for daily reading.

The purpose of committing to scripture reading is to keep you in God's word. God speaks to us through His word. The purpose of the scripture reading is not for in-depth study.

4. Bible Study

Bible study will consist of a lesson that has a scriptural text, questions relevant to the text and applications for daily living. The lesson is designed to be completed over the course of a week. There will be one lesson per week for six weeks. During the maintenance phase of Fit for Service, a lesson will be provided monthly to study prior to the next meeting which will be relevant to our theme and discussion. The purpose of this Bible study is not to replace studying for Sunday school lessons or other Bible study classes. The Bible study is intended to guide our thoughts toward Christian living in optimal health in mind, body and spirit.

5. Exercise

In 1 Corinthians 3:16 is says, "Don't you know that you yourselves are God's temple and God's Spirit lives in you?" We are the dwelling place for God. Our body is His home. Now ask yourself, what shape is God's house in? Are you ashamed of the size? How about what goes into His house? Is the dwelling place for God rested enough to be healthy? If your body needs nurturing and repair then it is time to fix it up. If your body is already fit then strive to improve God's dwelling place to maintain optimal health and fitness for service to the Kingdom.

Although Fit for Service wants you to commit to exercise, there is not a commitment to join or participate in any particular program or gym. **Physical exercise** is often defined as any bodily activity that enhances or maintains physical fitness and overall health. It is performed for many different reasons. These include strengthening muscles and the cardiovascular system, honing athletic skills, weight loss or maintenance and for enjoyment. Frequent and regular physical exercise boosts the immune system, and helps prevent the "diseases of affluence" such as heart disease, cardiovascular disease, Type 2 diabetes and obesity. Fit for Service addresses all areas of physical fitness that include

1) Food that we eat. The Fit for Service meal plan is designed to provide a balanced meal that provides proper nutrition. The plan is also to teach you how to make favorite meals healthier.

2) Physical activity is crucial to become fit. Even though a person does not over eat and maintains their weight is not an indicator that the person is physically fit. To get into optimal physical fitness requires movement regularly. Fit for Service recommends exercising three to five times a week for at least 30 minutes. There are a number of resources provided to help you plan your activities and teach you how to incorporate exercise into your daily routine.

3) Rest, sweet rest. Sleep is so important to maintaining our bodies. When you sleep the body can to refresh, replenish and

get ready for another day. However, in this 24/7 society, sleep and rest are often the most likely activities that are deprived. For many years it has been said that the body requires eight (8) hours of sleep each day. Fit for Service encourages sleep and rest naturally. With the pressures of the world today one is not allowed to slow down and prepare for sleep so many are dependent on sleeping aids. Fit for Service encourages relaxation and falling asleep naturally without the use of sleeping aids such as tranquilizers, alcohol or other substances.

4) Lifestyle habits are the activities you do on a regular basis. There are good habits and bad lifestyle habits that affect overall well-being and health. Bad lifestyle habits such as excess drinking of alcohol, illicit or prescription drug abuse, smoking, over eating, and a host of other habits. Examine yourself and you can determine whether your regular lifestyle is one pleasing and whether your body represents a temple where God will dwell. Fit for Service will address lifestyle habits that can lead to illness and encourage lifestyle behaviors that promote health.

6. Live the life

The final commitment is to live the life that learned. Remember that Rome was not built in a day. Fit for Service is not a quick weight loss plan or quick fix. Fit for Service is a program for life. This is not a program to start, complete in six weeks then move on to something else. The most important goal for any program designed to improve or teach a better way of life is to retain what was learned. In other words, **STAY FOCUSED; BRING SOMEONE ELSE ALONG AND KEEP THE CHANGE!**

FIT FOR SERVICE FORMS

The Fit for Service program is founded on commitments to change and setting goals. Goals can be met when there is a plan in place, and the plan is reviewed and evaluated at regular intervals. The forms in the Fit for Service program are designed for just that purpose. You will set a goal to accomplish by attending this program and write it down. We will help you to reach that goal by reviewing your plan one on one on a weekly basis. The maintenance phase of the program is designed to give you the tools to stay focused on reaching your goals through monthly evaluation during the meetings.

Commitment Form

This form is designed to keep you focused. You will record the information required daily. One side of is a food diary. You will record everything that you eat and drink. The second side of the page includes the commitments for Fit for Service. Each day you will record whether you have addressed each commitment for the program.

Personal Weight Record

This form is for you to maintain. Each week weigh yourself. Record the amount lost or gained and your goal. Keeping a written record will help you keep you focused on getting closer to your goal.

A number of articles, websites and information sheets are included in your workbook. Take the opportunity to read the articles and incorporate new practices into your lifestyle.

Guidelines for Healthy Eating

The guidelines listed below are the recommendations provided by the U. S. Health and Human Services Department

FOOD GROUPS TO ENCOURAGE

- Consume a sufficient amount of fruits and vegetables while staying within energy needs. Two cups of fruit and 2½ cups of vegetables per day are recommended for a reference 2,000-calorie intake, with higher or lower amounts depending on the calorie level.

- Choose a variety of fruits and vegetables each day. In particular, select from all five

Vegetable subgroups (dark green, orange, legumes, starchy

vegetables, and other

Vegetables) several times a week.

- Consume 3 or more ounce-equivalents of whole-grain products per day, with the rest of the recommended grains coming from enriched or whole-grain products. In general, at least half the grains should come from whole grains.

- Consume 3 cups per day of fat-free or low-fat milk or equivalent milk products.

FATS

- Consume less than 10 percent of calories from saturated fatty acids and less than 300 mg/day of cholesterol, and keep Trans fatty acid consumption as low as possible.

- Keep total fat intake between 20 to 35 percent of calories, with most fats coming from sources of polyunsaturated and monounsaturated fatty acids, such as fish, nuts, and vegetable oils.

- When selecting and preparing meat, poultry, dry beans, and milk or milk products, make choices that are lean, low-fat, or fat-free.

- Limit intake of fats and oils high in saturated and/or Trans fatty acids, and choose products low in such fats and oils.

CARBOHYDRATES

- Choose fiber-rich fruits, vegetables, and whole grains often.

- Choose and prepare foods and beverages with little added sugars or caloric sweeteners, such as amounts suggested by the USDA Food Guide and the DASH Eating Plan.

11

- Reduce the incidence of dental caries by practicing good oral hygiene and consuming sugar- and starch-containing foods and beverages less frequently.

SODIUM AND POTASSIUM

- Consume less than 2,300 mg (approximately 1 teaspoon of salt) of sodium per day.
- Choose and prepare foods with little salt. At the same time, consume potassium-rich foods, such as fruits and vegetables.

ALCOHOLIC BEVERAGES

- Those who choose to drink alcoholic beverages should do so sensibly and in moderation defined as the consumption of up to one drink per day for women and up to two drinks per day for men.
- Alcoholic beverages should not be consumed by some individuals, including those who cannot restrict their alcohol intake, women of childbearing age who may become pregnant, pregnant and lactating women, children and adolescents, individuals taking medications that can interact with alcohol, and those with specific medical conditions.
- Alcoholic beverages should be avoided by individuals engaging in activities that require attention, skill, or coordination, such as driving or operating machinery.

FOOD SAFETY

To avoid microbial food borne illness:

- Clean hands, food contact surfaces, and fruits and vegetables. Meat and poultry should not be washed or rinsed.
- Separate raw, cooked, and ready-to-eat foods while shopping, preparing, or storing foods.
- Cook foods to a safe temperature to kill microorganisms.
- Chill (refrigerate) perishable food promptly and defrost foods properly.
- Avoid raw (unpasteurized) milk or any products made from unpasteurized milk, raw or partially cooked eggs or foods containing raw eggs, raw or undercooked meat and poultry, unpasteurized juices, and raw sprouts.

Glycemic Index Meal Planning

The news has been inundated with information about the glycemic index of foods. Below is brief description and background information about glycemic index and meal planning. This section on glycemic index is to provide you with the basic information for understanding the concept.

What is the glycemic index?

The glycemic index, or GI, measures how a carbohydrate-containing food raises blood glucose. Foods are ranked based on how they compare to a reference food– either glucose or white bread. A food with a high GI raises blood glucose more than a food with a medium or low GI.

Meal planning with the GI involves choosing foods that have a low or medium GI. If eating a food with a high GI, you can combine it with low GI foods to help balance the meal. Examples of carbohydrate-containing foods with a low GI include dried beans and legumes (like kidney beans and lentils), all non-starchy vegetables and some starchy vegetables, most fruit, and many whole grain breads and cereals (like barley, whole wheat bread, rye bread, and all-bran cereal). Meats and fats don't have a GI because they do not contain carbohydrate.

What affects the GI of a food?
Fat and fiber tend to lower the GI of a food. As a general rule, the more cooked or processed a food, the higher the GI; however, this is not always true.

Below are a few specific examples of other factors that can affect the GI of a food:

- Ripeness and storage time – the more ripe a fruit or vegetable is, the higher the GI
- Processing – juice has a higher GI than whole fruit; mashed potato has a higher GI than a whole baked potato, stone ground whole wheat bread has a lower GI than whole wheat bread.
- Cooking method: how long a food is cooked (al dente pasta has a lower GI than soft-cooked pasta)

- Variety: converted long-grain white rice has a lower GI than brown rice but short-grain white rice has a higher GI than brown rice.

Other things to consider if using the GI:

- The GI value represents the type of carbohydrate in a food but says nothing about the amount of carbohydrate typically eaten. Portion sizes are still relevant for managing blood glucose and for losing or maintaining weight.
- The GI of a food is different when eaten alone than it is when combined with other foods. When eating a high GI food, you can combine it with other low GI foods to balance out the effect on blood glucose levels.
- Many nutritious foods have a higher GI than foods with little nutritional value. For example, oatmeal has a higher GI than chocolate. Use of the GI needs to be balanced with basic nutrition principles of variety for healthful foods and moderation of foods with few nutrients.

Is the GI a better tool than carbohydrate counting?

There is no one diet or meal plan that works for everyone. The important thing is to follow a meal plan that is tailored to personal preferences and lifestyle and helps achieve goals for reduction of risk of diabetes, hypertension, high cholesterol and weight management.

Note: The glycemic index of foods is used to monitor blood sugar values primarily in people who have been diagnosed with diabetes or pre-diabetes. For more information on glycemic index of foods and how to calculate refer to the American Diabetes Association website at www.ada.org.

Fit for Service Meal Planning for Weight Management

The Fit for Service meal plan is a well-balanced diet that includes all six food groups using the recommendations from the Food Guide Pyramid from the United States Dietary Association (USDA). This guide is not to meant to replace any recommendations for recommended by your physician or healthcare professional. For instance if you are taking certain medications such as Coumadin (warfarin) then you are aware that you are not to eat certain green leafy vegetables without consulting your physician.

The next few pages will include suggestions for managing the food choices because the key to managing your weight is also to balance caloric intake with the amount of calories burned through regular body functions and physical activity.

The Food Guide Pyramid
A Guide to Daily Food Choices

The Food Guide Pyramid is an outline of what to eat each day based on the Dietary Guidelines. It's not a rigid prescription but a general guide that lets you choose a healthful diet that's right for you.

The Pyramid calls for eating a variety of foods to get the nutrients you need and at the same time the right amount of calories to maintain healthy weight.

Use the Pyramid to help you eat better every day...the Dietary Guidelines way. Start with plenty of breads, cereals, rice, pasta, vegetables, and fruits. Add 2-3 servings from the milk group and 2-3 servings from the meat group. Remember to go easy on fats, oils, and sweets, the foods in the small tip of the Pyramid.

While sweets are allowed in the pyramid, we recommend that you eliminate sugar until you reach your goal. Salt and caffeine should also be considered off limits. Sugar does not have fat however, when sugar is digested unused energy from sugar is stored as fat.

Salt causes fluid retention which in turn causes the heart to work harder to pump blood to tissues. When the heart has to work harder to get blood throughout our body the blood pressure rises and the heart does not have ample time to rest. You get the picture; one scenario leads to another and over a period of time can lead to hypertension or other illnesses.

Caffeine is a stimulant. Caffeine is found in many soft drinks, coffee, tea, even some chocolate candy. Caffeine stimulates the body by constricting blood vessels making it harder for blood to go through. To keep blood circulating to our body the heart pumps harder thus increasing our heart rate which in turns pumps blood to throughout the body faster. When you get that jolt from a cup of coffee, you feel alert and ready to go! But over time the effects of caffeine on the body can be very harmful. There are a number of medications in the class of stimulants which many refer to as "speed" that are by prescription only or illegal. Many of us would not consider taking a drug that is in the class of a methamphetamine "meth" but did you not know that caffeine is in that class?

What Counts as One Serving?

The amount of food that counts as one serving is listed below. If you eat a larger portion, count it as more than 1 serving. For example, a dinner portion of spaghetti would count as 2 or 3 servings of pasta. Your notebook includes an article that gives a more vivid description of portion sizes. The pictorial description is useful if you are eating out or do not have a way of measuring the food that you are about to eat.

Be sure to eat at least the lowest number of servings from the five major food groups listed below. You need them for the vitamins, minerals, carbohydrates, and protein they provide. Just try to pick the lowest fat choices from the food groups. No specific serving size is given for the fats, oils, and sweets group because the message is USE SPARINGLY.

Milk, Yogurt, and Cheese		
1 cup of milk or yogurt	1 1/2 ounces of natural cheese	2 ounces of process cheese
Meat, Poultry, Fish, Dry Beans, Eggs, and Nuts		
2-3 ounces of cooked lean meat, poultry, or fish	1/2 cup of cooked dry beans, 1 egg, or 2 tablespoons of peanut butter count as 1 ounce of lean meat	
Vegetable		
1 cup of raw leafy vegetables	1/2 cup of other vegetables, cooked or chopped raw	3/4 cup of vegetable juice
Fruit		

1 medium apple, banana, orange	1/2 cup of chopped, cooked, or canned fruit	3/4 cup of fruit juice
Bread, Cereal, Rice, and Pasta (Starches)		
1 slice of bread	1 ounce of ready-to-eat cereal	1/2 cup of cooked cereal, rice, or pasta

While the food pyramid is a guideline to selecting food choices, the pyramid alone will not help you to lose excess weight. A successful weight loss plan is one in which calories burned is greater than calories consumed. Fit for Service has incorporated a food exchange list based on the serving sizes of the food pyramid to help you get a handle on the amount of calories required each day.

The meal plan with food exchanges is adopted from the American Diabetes Association Guidelines.

It is recommended that women start with a minimum of 1200 calories and men no less than 1500 calories per day.

FOOD EXCHANGES	NUMBER OF EXCHANGES								
	1200	1400	1500	1600	1800	2000	2200	2400	2600
Morning									
Lean Meat	1	1	1	1	2	2	2	2	2
Bread	1	1	2	2	3	3	4	4	4
Fruit	1	1	1	1	1	1	1	2	2
Milk	1	1	1	1	1	1	1	1	1
Fat	1	1	1	1	1	1	1	2	2
Midday									
Meat	2	2	2	2	2	2	2	2	2
Bread	2	2	2	3	3	4	4	5	5

FOOD EXCHANGES	NUMBER OF EXCHANGES								
	1200	1400	1500	1600	1800	2000	2200	2400	2600
*Vegetable	1	1	1	1	1	1	1	1	1
Fruit	1	1	1	1	1	1	1	1	1
Milk	½	½	½	½	½	½	½	½	½
Fat	1	1	1	1	1	2	3	3	3
Evening									
Lean Meat	2	2	2	2	3	3	3	3	3
Bread	2	4	4	4	4	4	4	4	5
Vegetable	1	1	1	2	2	2	2	2	3
Fruit	1	1	1	1	1	1	2	2	2
Milk	½	½	½	½	½	½	½	½	1
Fat	1	1	2	2	2	3	4	4	4
% Carbohydrate	55	55	55	55	55	55	55	55	55
% Protein	20	20	20	20	20	20	20	20	20
% Fat	25	25	25	25	25	25	25	25	25

*Vegetables listed are a daily minimum. Also, the plan setup is suggestive. Some people would rather eat 4-6 small meals a day rather than 3 large meals. The main point is to follow the exchange list for the amount of calories to eat in day.

Pregnant and nursing mothers consult your physician regarding following a particular meal plan.

Anyone with medical conditions such as diabetes, hypertension or other illnesses recommend that you consult your physician before beginning an exercise or weight loss program.

While there are a number of exchange lists available for reference the list above is a general guideline to help you stay focused. If you have access to the internet a number of programs are available online at no cost that will provide the caloric breakdown of foods individually. The lists will also provide the calories for restaurant and prepackaged meals. One program is The Daily Plate. The website address: www.thedailyplate.com.

Recording what, when and why you eat daily will help make you aware of the food consumed and monitor your success.
The chart below is a guide to the number of calories included in a food serving. Practice reading the food labels on all foods that you eat. The package label contains information about the food item and any additives used in the preparation.

Remember that the food exchange is based on standard serving size.

<h1 style="text-align:center"><u>Food Exchanges</u></h1>

Food Exchange	US Unit	Metric	Comments
Starches	80 Calories		15 g Carb., 3 g Protein, 1 g Fat
<ul><li>bread</li><li>breads, other</li><li>tortilla</li><li>crackers</li><li>cooked cereals</li><li>dry cereals, unsweetened</li><li>dry cereals, sweetened</li><li>dry flour or grain</li><li>pasta</li><li>rice</li><li>corn</li><li>popcorn</li><li>potato (small)</li><li>potato, mashed</li><li>sweet potato</li><li>squash, winter</li><li>cooked beans, peas, lentils (add 1 meat exchange)</li></ul>	1 slice 1 oz 1 (6") 4-6 (3/4 oz) 1/2 cup 3/4 cup 1/2 cup 3 Tbsp 1/2 cup 1/3 cup 1/2 cup 3 cups 1 (3 oz) 1/2 cup 1/3 cup 1 cup 1/2 cup	1 slice 30 g 1 (15 cm) 4-6 (20 g) 125 ml 175 ml 125 ml 45 ml 125 ml 80 ml 125 ml 720 ml 1 (85 g) 125 ml 80 ml 250 ml 125 ml	Most starches are a good source of B vitamins Choose whole grain foods such as 'all natural, 100% whole wheat' bread, pasta, tortillas, and brown rice, etc. for nutrients and fiber. Combine beans (starch & meat) with grains (starch) for their complimentary proteins and fiber Combine grains (starch) with milk (milk) or cheese (meat) to complement proteins.

23

Food Exchange	US Unit	Metric	Comments
			Add additional fat exchanges for starchy foods prepared with fat.
Vegetables	25 Calories		5 g Carb., 2 g Protein
• raw vegetables • cooked vegetables • tomato or vegetable juice	1 cup 1/2 cup 1/2 cup	250 ml 125 ml 125 ml	Choose more dark green leafy and deep yellow vegetables such as spinach, broccoli, carrots, and peppers.
Fruit	60 Calories		15 g Carb.
• fresh fruit • melon (cubes) • canned fruit • dried fruit • fruit juice	1 small 12 oz (1 cup) 1/2 cup 1/4 cup 1/2 cup	1 small 360 g (250 ml) 125 ml 60 ml 125 ml	Choose whole fruits for fiber Choose citrus fruits such as oranges, grapefruits, or tangerines
Meat & Substitutes	35-145 Calories		7 g Protein, 0-13 g Fat

Food Exchange	US Unit	Metric	Comments
• meat, poultry, fish • cheese • cottage cheese • egg • peanut butter • tofu • cooked beans, peas, lentils (add 1 starch)	1 oz 1 oz 1/4 cup 1 1.5 Tbsp 4 oz (1/2 cup) 1/2 cup	30 g 30 g 60 ml 1 22 ml 115 g (125 ml) 125 ml	Choose leaner meats such as chicken, fish, and lean cuts of meat; add fat exchange for higher fat meats and substitutes. Remove skin from poultry. Limit frying or adding fat. Have 2 servings of fish per week for Omega 3 fatty acid.
Milk	80-150 Calories		12 g Carb., 8 g Protein, 0-8 g Fat
• milk • yogurt	1 cup 1 cup	250 ml 250 ml	Choose lower fat milks; add fat exchange for higher fat milk.
Fat	45 Calories		5 g Fat
• oil • mayonnaise • cream cheese • salad dressing • peanuts • avocado • butter or margarine	1 tsp 1 tsp 1 Tbsp 1 Tbsp 10 1/8 1 tsp	5 ml 5 ml 15 ml 15 ml 10 1/8 5 ml	Eat less saturated fat such as animal fat found in fatter meat, cheeses, butter, and

Food Exchange	US Unit	Metric	Comments
• higher fat exchange (additional)	1 exchange	1 exchange	tropical oils (eg: palm). Also eat less hydrogenated fat, or trans-fats. Consume mono-unsaturated fat and moderate poly-unsaturated fat. Check Nutrition Facts on food labels; 5 g Fat = 1 Fat exchange.
Sweets	Calories vary		15 g Carb., Protein & Fat varies
• ice cream • cookies • syrup • jam or jelly • sugar • pudding • muffin or cupcake	1/2 cup 2 small 1 Tbsp 1 Tbsp 2 Tbsp 1/4 cup 1/2 small	125 ml 2 small 15 ml 15 ml 30 ml 60 ml 1/2 small	Choose sweets sparingly Can be substituted for a 1 Starch, Fruit, or Milk exchange. Add 1 or 2 Fat exchanges for sweets containing fat.

FREE FOODS

The food items listed below are low in calories and contain very little if any nutrients. However, in moderation they can be included in your meal plan. Many of these items contain artificial sweeteners. Since artificial sweeteners are controversial in their usefulness to weight management, Fit for Service recommends use of artificial sweeteners in moderation.

Condiments	Drinks	Fruit	Sugar Substitutes
Ketchup (1 tbsp) Horseradish Fat Free Cream Cheese (1 tbsp) Mustard Pickles dill or - unsweetened Fat-free margarine Fat-free sour cream Picante sauce (1 tbsp) Vinegar Nonstick vegetable spray such as Pam *Seasonings	Bouillon or broth (low fat and low sodium) Carbonated drinks (sugar free) Carbonated water Club soda Cocoa powder (unsweetened) Coffee/tea Drink mixes (sugar free) Tonic water, sugar free	Cranberries (unsweetened) ½ cup Rhubarb (unsweetened) ½ cup	Gelatin, sugar free Chewing gum Jam/jelly or all fruit (2tsp) Pancake syrup (sugar free) Sugar substitutes

*Sodium is a seasoning. Ensure that you read your labels for sodium content. Sodium can be hidden in foods such as ketchup, diet carbonated beverages and seasonings. The recommendation is to limit sodium to 400 milligrams per serving for a food item and the recommended daily allowance of sodium is 3000 milligrams per day. Please note for those who are on sodium restrictions by your physician, follow the amount prescribed.

WHAT IS THE RIGHT AMOUNT OF CALORIES FOR ME?

The amount of calories required each day is determined by the Basal Metabolic Rate (BMR). The basal metabolic rate, or **BMR**, is the minimum calorific requirement needed to sustain life in a resting individual. BMR is described as the amount of energy (measured in calories) that sustains life.

There are a number of factors that can affect the BMR. Typically with age, BMR or the metabolism slows. It is harder to maintain weight or to lose weight. The BMR can be affected by genetics, gender, age and body surface area. Other influences are exercise, body temperature, outside temperature and diet.

The BMR can be calculated to determine the number of calories required to maintain, lose or gain weight. The total daily energy expenditure (TDEE) is the total number of calories that your body expends in 24 hours, including all activities. TDEE is also known as your "maintenance level". Use the formula below to calculate your BMR and current calorie needs. In order to lose weight it has been shown that you must remove at least 500 calories from your daily caloric intake to lose 1-2 pounds per week. A pound is equal to 3500 calories.

The Harris-Benedict formula (BMR based on total body weight)

The Harris Benedict equation is a calorie formula using the factors of height, weight, age, and sex to determine basal metabolic rate (BMR). This makes it more accurate than determining calorie needs based on total bodyweight alone. The only variable it does not take into consideration is lean body mass. Therefore, this equation will be very accurate in all but the extremely muscular can underestimate caloric needs and the extremely obese will overestimate caloric needs.

Men: BMR = 66 + (13.7 X wt in kg) + (5 X ht in cm) - (6.8 X age in years)

Women: BMR = 655 + (9.6 X wt in kg) + (1.8 X ht in cm) - (4.7 X age in years)

Note: 1 inch = 2.54 cm.
1 kilogram = 2.2 lbs.

Example:
You are female
You are 30 yrs old
You are 5' 6 " tall (167.6 cm)
You weigh 120 lbs. (54.5 kilos)
Your BMR = 655 + 523 + 302 - 141 = **1339 calories/day**

Now that you know your BMR, you can calculate TDEE by multiplying your BMR by your activity multiplier from the chart below:

Activity Multiplier
Sedentary = BMR X 1.2 (little or no exercise, desk job)
Lightly active = BMR X 1.375 (light exercise/sports 1-3 days/wk)
Mod. active = BMR X 1.55 (moderate exercise/sports 3-5 days/wk)
Very active = BMR X 1.725 (hard exercise/sports 6-7 days/wk)

Extr. active = BMR X 1.9 (hard daily exercise/sports & physical job or 2X day training, i.e marathon, contest etc.)

Example:
Your BMR is 1339 calories per day
Your activity level is moderately active (work out 3-4 times per week)
Your activity factor is 1.55
Your TDEE = 1.55 X 1339 = **2075 calories/day**

Again, you must reduce your normal caloric intake by 500 calories per day to lose weight. In addition to eating less, extra calories are burned through exercise. The chart below was adopted by the American Council on Exercise (ACE) and the American Diabetes Association. The chart an provides proximate number of calories burned with activity for average 160 or 180 pound person for 30 minutes unless noted otherwise.

Activity & Calories Burnt	160 lbs	180 lbs
Aerobics (per minute)	9.8	11.1
Basketball	300	339
Bike riding (10 mph)	219	246
Golf (pulling clubs)	186	210
Jogging	372	417
Skating (ice and roller)	237	264
Skiing (snow and water)	228	255
Swimming (moderate pace)	309	348
Tennis	237	267
Walking (briskly)	261	291
Weight Training	261	294
Fast Dancing	193	223

Activity & Calories Burnt	160 lbs	180 lbs
Gardening (planting, weeding)	150	180
Mowing the lawn (with a push mower)	200	230
Raking leaves	135	185
Washing/waxing a car	112	142
Jumping Rope	280	310
Flying a kite	105	135
Housecleaning	150	180

As you can see, opportunities to exercise and burn the extra 500 calories per day to lose weight can be fun and a part of the daily routine.

KEEPING THE CHANGE

The Fit for Service eating plan will help you reach your desired weight goal and is designed to help you maintain the weight as well. That is why this section is entitled KEEP THE CHANGE. Fit for Service is a lifestyle. When the principles of eating and being fit physically, mentally and spiritually are practiced daily it is considered a permanent part of your being. Once you reach your optimal weight and live an abundant Christian life why would anyone want to go back to being the old person?

After you reach the desired weight goal using following the exchange plan, immediately move to the next column to maintain your weight. For example, if you use the 1200 calorie per day plan to reach your optimal weight, then once you reach your desired weight the ideal plan to maintain the weight will be to move to the 1400 calorie plan. Now you must remember that once the goal is reached everything that you did to reach the goal must be maintained. That includes exercising.

FIT FOR SERVICE BIBLE STUDY

Principles of Christian Living

What's the purpose of living a Christian lifestyle? Choosing to make Jesus Christ the Lord of our life changes our lifestyle dramatically. Friendships, activities, and even health issues receive careful evaluation. The lesson will be taken from Romans Chapters 12. Read each chapter then answer the questions associated. Pace your study throughout the week and apply the reading to your goal for participating in Fit for Service.

Paul is the author of Romans. Theologians and historians note that the book or Romans was probably written in A.D. 57. Rome was well established by the time the book was written. The church was probably large as there were more than a million people living in Rome at the time.

Romans 12:1-2.

[1]Therefore, I urge you, brothers, in view of God's mercy, to offer your bodies as living sacrifices, holy and pleasing to God—this is your spiritual act of worship. [2]Do not conform any longer to the pattern of this world, but be transformed by the renewing of your mind. Then you will be able to test and approve what God's will is— his good, pleasing and perfect will.

1. What is the meaning of offering your bodies as living sacrifices?

____

____

____

Paul wrote in a language that the people could understand and make reference. Since the people did not have the "New Testament" the New Testament Christians referred to the Old Testament to teach others Jesus Christ.

2. Read the following passages and write your thoughts about the types of offerings that were required under the law: Lev 1; 6:8-13; 8:18-21; 16:24, Lev 2; 6:14-23, Lev 3; 7:11-34, Lev 4:1-5:13; 6:24-30; 8:14-17; 16:3-22, Lev 5:14-6:7; 7:1-6.

____

____

____

____

____

____

Because Christ sacrificed and died on the cross and with His blood washed away our sins. We no longer have to make the sacrifices as outlined in Leviticus.

 The world today is accessible instantly. We can access events as they happen. The media is a huge giant that provides constant stimulation about what is going on in the world. Not only do the media keep us informed, the media dictates who society likes, dislikes, what we eat, wear, drive and watch. Why?

____

____

____

____

____

3. What is the command for us in Romans 12:2? What are some examples of confirmations to society today that is good for you? What are some examples of confirmations that are not in the best interest of a Christian living in Christ?

____

____

____

____

____

 Read Romans 12: 9-21. These verses provide instruction for how we are to treat each other. List some of the commandments that you find more challenging. What makes these

commandments more difficult for you than others?

____

____

____

____

____

____

Read Galatians 5: 22-26 and Galatians 6:1-10. What principles of Christian living are noted in these verses?

____

____

____

____

____

When faced with the challenges of living by these commandments consider what Jesus would do. Philippians' 4:13 reads: I can do all things through Christ that strengthens me. Ask God to help you get rid of the challenges that keep you from treating everyone as we are commanded.

Overcoming Temptation

"No temptation has overtaken you but such as is common to man; and God is faithful who will not allow you to be tempted beyond what you are able, but with the temptation will provide the way to escape also, that you may be able to endure it.
1Corinthians 10:13

1Corthians 10:13 affirms that God is faithful to us. In what ways can you think of in which God has helped you overcome temptation?

____

____

____

____

____

____

We are all at risk of being tempted to do deeds unbecoming of a Christian. God loves us and wants us to be as our perfect example, Jesus Christ. The Christian needs to understand that God does not lead us to sin. The Apostle James condemns the attitude of blaming God for tempting circumstances (James 1:13-15). God may test His children, which is done in order to purify and strengthen them, but He does not lead them into sin. Without exception, sin results when temptation comes at a weak moment in one's life. There is no one to blame but self.

Read Matthew 4:1-11. How many times did the devil tempt Jesus? _______________________.   What is the significance of the knowing that Jesus was fasting?

____

____

____

____

____

____

When do you feel most vulnerable to your temptations (overeating, drinking, shopping, etc.)?

____

____

What is your most difficult temptation to overcome and what are you doing to rid yourself of the desire for this temptation?

____

____

____

____

____

What can you do to overcome your temptations?

Read Psalms 119: 11. When God's Word becomes an integral part of the believer's life, it fortifies that person against temptation's power. So then, what is needed to overcome temptation?

Read 2Corinthians 2:11 and Ephesians 6: 11-17. What are the unique characteristics of these verses in overcoming temptation?

As Christians, we are commanded to help each other overcome temptation as written in Ephesians 4: 15-16. God's promises to not allow us to be tempted beyond our capacity to withstand the temptation and he also promises to provide us with an outlet to break free from the temptation. Break free from whatever temptations are preventing you from being fit for service to the kingdom!

PRAYER

A dictionary definition of Prayer is the act of addressing a god or spirit for the purpose of worship or petition. Specific forms of this may include praise, requesting guidance or assistance, confessing sins, as an act of reparation or an expression of one's thoughts and emotions. The words used in prayer may take the form of intercession, a hymn, incantation, words of gratItude, or a spontaneous utterance in the person's praying words. Praying can be done in public, as a group, or in private.

The Christian definition of prayer is the act of talking to God. God expects for us to pray to Him without ceasing. An effective prayer enriches our life. Jeremiah 33:3 tells reads, "Call to me and I will answer you and tell you great and unsearchable things you do not know."

We pray for a lot of reasons. We pray to God for guidance, healing and grace. Read John 14: 13. What is the most important reason to pray?

____

____

____

____

According to Matthew 6:33 what types of prayer will God answer?

____

____

____

____

____

____

Read 1 Corinthians 6:20. Can you relate this scripture to Fit for

Service?

____

____

____

____

____

As Christians, we have the right to pray to God. Not just during
times of need but also during good times. We should include
prayers of thanksgiving and just to praise to God for all that He has
done for us.

Read Psalms 107: 19-20. What is significant about this verse in regards to praying to God?

____

____

____

____

____

____

John 14:13 Jesus tells us to call His name when we pray. What is so unique about calling the name of Jesus when we pray based on the John 14: 13? What about John 15: 16, John 16:23 and John 16:24?

____

____

____

____

____

____

Read 1John 3:22. What two steps are outlined in this passage that we must do to receive answers to our prayers?

____

____

____

____

KNOWING GOD

 I am the "good shepherd: an I know My own, and My own know Me, even as the Father knows Me and I know the Father; and I lay down My life for the sheep. John 10:16

Christians are so wonderfully blessed, sometimes just thinking of the words of Jesus can make you just get goose bumps all over. This lesson will help you mediate on God's love for us and knowing God. A Christian must know and recognize the presence of God in his life.

Read Psalms 139:1-3. From this verse, what does God know about you?

____

____

____

____

____

____

Explain how you feel knowing that God knows you fully?

____

____

____

____

____

____

God is everywhere. When you have the love of God, you know and feel His presence in your life. Read John 10:27 and 2Timothy 2: 19. How do these verses relate to what God knows and cares for?

____

____

____

____

____

God knows us and we should know Him and marvel at the greatness. He provides for the whole world and knows everything! That knowledge should provide comfort that God knows the struggles, triumphs of each and every person in the world. What an awesome God!

JOY

"A joyful heart is good medicine, but a broken spirit dries up the bones. Proverbs 17:22

We all have days when we just can't seem to find anything to be joyful about. Even though we have the all of God's blessings and goodness around us everywhere we can't seem to focus on anything but what is not going well, pitfalls boredom. During these moments where there is no joy we are vulnerable to the cares of the world. This lesson will provide scripture references of how God's people handled joylessness and what God's plan is for us. Once we learn to renew our joy, we can help others find joy in the love of God because joy is contagious.

Read Proverbs 23:29. What are your thoughts about the verse and the joyless living described?

____

____

____

____

____

____

Read Isaiah 24: 11. What happened to the joy of the people?

____

____

____

____

____

____

Read Psalm 126:6. We have the promise of Joy. What does this verse say about the change from sorrow to joy?

____

____

____

____

____

____

Joy is contagious! We all know someone who is happy and gay every time you see them. No matter what problems abound the person can still be joyful. As Christians we are to be sincere and joyful as well. Sometimes we can be shy or afraid of the joy that we experience.

Read Matthew 28:8. What is wrong with the joy described in this verse?

____

____

____

____

____

____

Often parents will describe a child as "my pride and joy." That statement is made because the child brings pleasure and satisfaction. Now sometimes this statement is used to describe other trinkets and treasures for a man it may be his car and for a woman it could be diamonds. But whatever the treasure is we take pride in talking about it, taking care of it and making sure that the treasure has all of its needs met. Does that description seem in anyway familiar to how God takes care of us? _______________________

Have you ever thought of God as our "pride and Joy"?

____

Read Deuteronomy 26:11. Discuss your thought about joy and a
relationship with God.

____

____

____

____

____

____

Now, read Psalms 84:1-2. Describe the joy of these verses.

____

____

____

____

____

____

We anxiously wait for grand openings, weddings, graduations and
the birth of babies. As the end nears and we know that we will be
able to experience the event we are filled with excitement like a
child waiting for Christmas morning. Can you imagine what the day
will be like when we get to be with God in glory? Jesus is preparing
a home for us with Him and when the time is right we will be
welcomed there. And in heaven, we will then know the magnitude
of joy that is reserved for those who love God.

Living an Abundant Life

It is a common misconception among non-Christians that the Christian life is boring. Christians are thought to be dull, humorless just plain people. Christians have encouraged the misconception that being a Christian is boring because to mis-instructions. Many Christians have long been taught that almost every activity except for work and attending church was a sin. A Christian should not live life in fear of committing sin but by the principles outlined for us in the Bible on how we are to love God and mankind. When we are living in fear and not understanding the full meaning of God's plan for our lives, we miss the whole meaning of living abundantly.

Read John 10: 10

The primary reason Christ came as a man to this earth was to teach us how to live abundant, fulfilled lives. Restate John 10:10 in your own words. What does this verse mean to you?

____

____

____

____

____

____

How is the Christian to live his life?   What are we no longer commanded to do?

____

____

____

____

____

____

Just because a Christian exercises self-control does not mean life is boring, underprivileged, and unrewarding. A Christian life is ultimately more exciting, successful, and satisfying than most human beings can imagine!   Do some research of scriptures in the Bible that describe the abundant life of a Christian. What makes the lives of these people abundant from your perspective? Is it about the money?

____

____

____

____

____

____